Beyond Negotiation

Beyond Negotiation

Redeeming Customer–Supplier Relationships

JOHN A. CARLISLE
TRANSFORM
Individual and Organisation Development, Sheffield, UK

and

ROBERT C. PARKER
Parker Management Associates, Wheaton, Illinois, USA

JOHN WILEY & SONS
Chichester • New York • Brisbane • Toronto • Singapore

Library of Congress Cataloging in Publication Data:
Carlisle, John A.
  Beyond negotiation / John A. Carlisle and Robert C. Parker.
    p.   cm.
  Bibliography: p.
  Includes index.
  ISBN 0 471 92203 X
  1. Industrial procurement. 2. Negotiation in business.
I. Parker, Robert C. II. Title.
HD39.5.C37   1989
658.8'02—dc19   88-27014
                                           CIP

British Library Cataloguing in Publication Data:
Carlisle, John A.
  Beyond negotiation.
  1. Purchasing. Behavioural aspects
  I. Title II. Parker, Robert C.
  658.7'2

  ISBN 0 471 92203 X

Typeset by Acorn Bookwork, Salisbury
Printed in Great Britain by St. Edmundsbury Press, Bury St. Edmunds

Contents

Foreword

In 1976, Atlas Door Corporation was formed, and in the ensuing years became a very successful company. I am always asked what was the secret of our success? What did we do different?

One of the more significant procedures I implemented at our inception was how to establish a relationship with suppliers. Since we were a small company, just starting out, our credit lines were limited and there was no leverage as the volume of our orders was small. It became evident that the only way we could get the delivery, quality and price we needed was to treat our suppliers as partners, making sure we explained our needs and our goals to them. By making them an integral member of our team we were able to get the best price and delivery possible, thereby establishing the short delivery our customers required, which was never available before. In addition, since our suppliers were part of our team, we did not have to stock large quantities of inventory. They made sure our orders were filled on time. They also used their expertise to provide us cost-saving designs and methods. Our component in this relationship was to allow them to make a fair profit and to meet the payment terms we had agreed upon. This developed a strong bond which was one of the secrets that allowed us to become a leader in our industry and set the pace for the rest of the competition to follow.

Beyond Negotiation is the first complete book which addresses the importance of the customer–supplier partnership. It carefully and thoroughly explains how to achieve and maintain a successful relationship to the benefit of both parties. Whether you purchase for a newly created or Fortune 500 company, in either the service or manufacturing industry, this text should be required reading.

It sheds light on and exposes one of the "secrets" of success of Atlas Door Corporation.

JOEL GOLDSCHEIN

Joel Goldschein is the visionary who founded and pushed Atlas Door Corporation in Edison, New Jersey, through ten straight years of 15% average annual growth in an industry growing only one third that fast. In recent years, the firm's pre-tax earnings have been 20% of sales, which is about five times the industry average. Atlas was debt-free and the number one performer in its industry when recently sold to the Masco Corporation in Detroit.

Joel's core strategy, which proved remarkably successful, was to respond to the customer's needs for special doors (for factories, aircraft hangers, shopping centers, etc.) faster than anyone else in the industry. As a crucial part of this strategy he selected key suppliers whom he could trust to respond within his tight customer promises, and committed himself to buy only from them as long as they performed as agreed. They performed, Atlas performed, and the rest of Joel's story is told in the *Harvard Business Review* of July/August, 1988.

Preface

Because the natural resources of the earth are not equally bestowed on all peoples, and the artisan skills to transform those materials into useful products do not spring up equally in all places, it has been necessary from very early times for humans to engage in the process of determining how to share something scarce between them. Thus, buying and selling are among the oldest activities of mankind. It was these activities, in fact, which gave rise to the very first need for a writing system in order to complete the buy–sell transaction when the two parties were distanced from one another. You can easily picture the transition from the clay tokens described in the caption to the illustration overleaf to the seals of the Mediterranean traders, and thence to the contracts of our modern world.

Because humans are inclined to look after their own needs first and foremost, this process of sharing carries with it many hazards to peaceful coexistence with our neighbors. As technology has made life progressively more complex by increasing the alternatives available to each of us, this process of sharing has played an important role in determining our relationship with many of the new and newly important constituencies in our lives.

In two lifetimes of dealing with these constituencies, and especially while training over 3000 negotiators to deal with their own, the authors separately have observed various patterns of behavior and strategies which tended to produce dissatisfaction, distrust and less than optimal use of those resources being shared. After all, Immanuel Kant tells us that

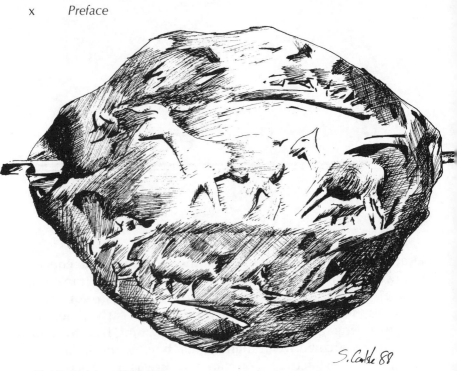

S. Carlisle 88

Clay bulla (circa 3300 BC)

A clay bulla *is both a record of early trade and a key to the first writing system. Each shipment of merchandise included a hollow clay* bulla *containing clay tokens that symbolized the goods being delivered. The surface was marked with notches corresponding to the number of tokens inside and impressed with the sender's seal, making the transaction official. The recipient would break open the* bulla *and compare the tokens with the notches, to make sure that neither shipment nor "invoice" had been tampered with.*

The bullae *and the clay tablets were important forerunners of methods for dealing with* **trust**, *which is an enduring theme of this book.*

in order to understand the other person's actions, we must look to their motives. John Carlisle saw this inefficient behavior as rooted in the organizational culture and the psychology of the individual, particularly in their conscious and unconscious motives. This conclusion was totally in keeping with his long experience in the development of business relationships among major European firms. Bob Parker saw it rooted more in the competitive and environmental factors bearing on the decision process, in keeping with his long experience in the making of such decisions as a purchasing executive for Ford Motor Company and International Harvester.

When we began working together in 1982 on a workshop designed by John for developing the negotiating skills of industrial buyers, we began to suspect that we were both right, but each of us had only half the story. In 1984 we decided to put all the pieces together in order to share our conclusions with anyone in the business of buying or selling. We particularly wanted to share any useful insights we have gained over the years from seeing behavior which was especially effective at persuading one party to do things for the other which they were not doing for just anyone.

While these insights will be useful for individuals on both sides of the buy–sell interaction, the book is written largely from the buyer's perspective, because it is the customer firm that is best positioned to take most of the recommended initiatives. This book will illuminate those basic influences which are eternally at work between customer firms and supplier firms and which play powerful, but too often unseen, roles in the decisions taken and the benefits enjoyed by both parties. In a nutshell, it is about *interdependent relationships*— and all that this really means today.

The writing of this book has been a journey which we undertook thinking we were the only ones going in that direction; but the delightful and unexpected truth is that, as we explored the path, we met so many fellow travelers and trailblazers. Although at times we have felt somewhat travel-weary there have been other times when we have been reinvigorated by bumping into the writing of an unsuspected companion who is touched by the same insights and who sees the same course which needs to be charted.

Two particular kindred spirits are Robert Hayes and Steven Wheelwright, who have written so very clearly about the role of manufacturing in the positioning of the whole organization for competitive advantage—including the need to examine new kinds of relationships. The *Harvard Business Review* and *Wall Street Journal* in the USA and *The Financial Times* in England consistently provided refreshing publications in which familiar names kept cropping up. In addition to Hayes and Wheelwright, there was Wickham Skinner, Rosabeth Kantor, Frank

Price, The IMP Project Group and Ivor Morgan. The Massachusetts Institute of Technology was an essential staging-post, especially in the total quality area and in the studies of the automobile industry.

The three figures who really dominated our thinking were, however, the uncompromising W. Edwards Deming, whose messages on quality leadership were consistently reinforced by our findings; Dr Bernard Lievegoed of the NPI in Holland, who speaks and writes so profoundly about people and organizations and the way they develop; and, standing like a Colossus over all we did, was Rudolf Steiner, whose works, often expressed through the NPI, provided the vital human development dimension that guided the essential philosophical framework to our final thoughts. We too often lose sight of the wonder of human potential when we are drawn into the machinations of organizations, and we need to be reminded, as Steiner reminds us again and again, that we all have a contribution to make and a larger destiny to fulfil.

It is also clear that the best thinking about work and organizations has passed from the academic to the worker in the organization—at all sorts of levels—and it is time this was acknowledged. When we look back at the courageous, insightful actions people in organizations take to help those organizations, and at the deep wisdom they often display at the work they do (when they have the appropriate leadership) then it is also clear that they are the real contributors to this tide of change sweeping us towards excellence. It is these people who provided the greatest delight and refreshment to us on our journey, and we are humbled and grateful.

Finally, John Carlisle's colleagues in Transform helped a great deal in giving shape to some of the key concepts. These often appeared in the forms of challenges to go back to basics; which are much appreciated now, although seldom enjoyed at the time. But then, what are colleagues for?

Introduction

MANUFACTURING, THE CINDERELLA INDUSTRY IN THE WEST

The manufacturing onslaught from the Pacific Basin over the last two decades has seriously damaged Europe and the USA. Home markets have been taken over in brown goods, automobiles, motorcycles and microchips at an alarming rate. More than a few manufacturing firms have been put out of business, sometimes through illegal dumping but mostly because they were simply uncompetitive in either price or quality. Others, sadly, just rolled over and died (the British motorcycle industry is a good example), leaving Japanese or other Pacific-Basin multinationals to enter and take their place.

At the same time this invasion may have just been the kick up the backside that our industries needed.

Reactions from Britain and the USA have been different. The Americans typically have fought back, at times blindly, at times crudely; but they have fought back. They have examined their adversaries from the East and produced careful studies and insightful books on Japanese organizations, as well as savagely critical and over-the-top analyses such as *The Japanese Conspiracy* (Wolf, 1983). At the same time, however, more-balanced observers have concluded that the *enemy is us*, and that the time has come to put our own house in order in the areas of quality, cost and consumer attention. The great quality gurus at last were listened to—especially Deming, Crosby and Juran—and that industrial Isaiah, Tom Peters, began to find more comfort

1

in his investigations; although not nearly enough to satisfy his passion for excellence.

In Britain, the reaction was much more low key, and in a lot of cases, wholly ineffectual. Mrs Thatcher's Conservative government, in particular, has been less than encouraging, giving the impression that manufacturing had had its day and that Britain was now a confirmed service nation—primarily of financial services. So the manufacturing base continued to erode, and the engineers continued their emigration—although some of the very best stayed in Britain and struggled on against high interest rates, short-term investment and an economic climate conducive to imports—at a time when the demand for consumer goods is higher than it has ever been. Green-field sites and economic assistance were given to cash-rich Japanese companies to set up in the more deprived areas of the country, while British initiatives struggled for investment. To be fair, however, the British government did make some attempts to encourage industry, but how substantial were they? Information Technology Year came and went, as did Industry Year in 1986, and still Britain remains insufficiently competitive.

So, it is not just the government that is to blame; it has after all provided the country with the National Quality Campaign out of the Department of Trade and Industry. But even the leaders of that effort are quoted as saying in the *Computer Weekly* of September 10, 1987, that "Quality Control is about to become a key concern of UK industrial management." *About to become!* This was 1987, when the manufacturing walls had been breached for over ten years, because even the British consumer, that most supine of customers, had given up on many British manufactured goods because the quality had been awful for so long! And now we get a statement of the obvious, which is not only outdated but also incomplete, as it is *total* quality that should be the key concern, not quality control. How long does it take to at least ask the right question?

We believe that manufacturing is vital to wealth creation, and agree with G. W. Runciman (a member of the Securities and Investment Board) in the 1987 *London Review of Books* when he states his concern that "financial services are not only parasitical on, but may be destructive of, the extractive and manufacturing industries *which alone generate wealth which is* 'real' . . ." (authors' emphasis). So we are disturbed at the extent of the manufacturing decline and feel it has been unnecessary. We share the frustration of people like Myron Tribus, late of MIT, who insists, quite rightly, that if manufacturing leadership had listened to Deming and his quality message even ten years ago we would not have suffered such a dramatic decline.

Deming, the man who is revered in Japan for transforming their manufacturing, who taught them that higher quality meant lower costs, and whose methods (along with Shewhart and Juran) helped accelerate American arms production to miraculous levels in the Second World War, and who has been hammering at the consciousness of Western manufacturing for 25 years, has been, until recently, largely ignored in the West. Instead we have looked at too many instant solutions provided by high-tech innovations, "clever" people, centralization or decentralization, differentiation strategies and so on, when the keys to manufacturing competitiveness lay in fact in quality processes for quality products, and quality relationships to release quality potential.

Despite all this frustration, however, we do see light at the end of the tunnel, for our decline is an "adjustment process." Some of our client companies are really paying attention to quality processes and relationships, and they are listening more carefully to the customer and to their employees. Some are even listening to their suppliers. As a result, they are becoming more competitive. We hope to accelerate this process by looking at one aspect of the relationships arena, the industrial buyer–seller relationship, which we believe is one of the last pieces of the jigsaw to fall into place—one of the last great frontiers for improving productivity. Getting this right is one of the vital keys to a competitive future.

In the following chapters, we shall explore the process of influencing the performance of individuals and firms who supply goods or services and identify those behaviors which have proved to be successful in improving the long-term benefit for both buyer and seller. This will make visible certain implicit structural and psychological factors which shape the reaction of one person to another, especially those that apply when two parties are engaged in the process of negotiation.

A key question is this: is what senior management is doing

when determining how best to utilize suppliers to meet their own customers' needs better than what their competitors are doing to meet those needs? This particular decision process can have a very significant impact on the firm's ability to compete effectively, because purchased materials and services are frequently the firm's largest on-going operating cost—even greater than the cost of labor in many manufacturing firms. Add the opportunity for that large purchased portion of the product to impact directly on utility or reliability, and it is apparent that the suppliers' impact on the ultimate consumer decision can be substantial.

We have observed that the dawning of the Information Age is creating a unique hazard to the procurement decision process by intensifying the feeling, which many in the Industrial Age held, that suppliers are merely cogs in the production machinery. Parallel with the decreasing frequency of person-to-person communication, as a result of growing computer-to-computer data transmission, there is an increasing risk that managers in customer firms will become even less conscious of their suppliers' clearly felt needs. Because they no longer have to face the supplier personally, it is easier to suggest a wholly self-centred course of action which fails to consider the supplier's needs. There is a great danger that they will confuse the high level of communication with a high level of relating—but the truth is they may be treating the supplier merely as a more sophisticated cog in a more sophisticated production machine.

BUYING AND SELLING AS AN ONGOING RELATIONSHIP

The kind of buying and selling we shall address is decidedly *not* similar to buying the weekly groceries, or even making a large individual consumer purchase, like an automobile, or a house. In those cases, the decision is being taken by the owner of the funds, rather than by an agent; the benefit is limited to the satisfaction provided by the goods or services themselves, and the transaction is one-of-a-kind, with little likelihood of it being repeated between the same parties.

We shall be talking about purchases of goods and services

which constitute only a step in the process of reaching the intended benefit, i.e. a profit to all the firms in the manufacturing chain who collectively succeed in meeting the consumers' needs better than anyone else. We will be working at the fundamental interpersonal level on the question of what really influences people during this process to become more responsive and supportive.

Beyond negotiation means dealing with the reality of embarking on a long-term, continuous relationship, rather than any short-term, one-of-a-kind interaction. Thus the concepts presented here have application in almost all interpersonal activities where one party desires to influence the behavior of the other over time. Our very specific goal, however, is to provide tools which meet the special needs of those who, on behalf of their organization, are responsible for large sums of money and for securing the greatest possible long-term value for the funds in their charge. So we expect that industrial buyers, and their managers in manufacturing firms, will find this book especially helpful, along with those who sell to them.

COOPERATION WORKS

Our thesis is simple to describe, though a great deal more difficult to put into practice. *Cooperation between industrial users and sellers is a far more powerful strategy for making them both more profitable in the long term than any adversarial approach yet devised.* If customer and supplier firms can recognize their common ground in a shared interest in capturing the consumer sale which actually nourishes them both, it should be possible for them to work creatively and effectively together to capture that sale for "their" product.

In the Western world, unfortunately, the opposite tends to happen at the interface between buyers and sellers in most manufacturing chains. Both parties seem to spend their energies too often in sophisticated forms of haggling in hopes of making their own piece of that transaction pie larger than the one received by the other party in the "win–lose" approach. The Japanese long ago recognized that the real adversary of both parties in this transaction is not even present at that moment i.e. the competition. They realize that these two parties would do better to work intimately together to make their product more attractive to the consumer who, after all, will make the actual choice to support both, or neither, of them.

This consumer orientation is the "common ground" for success, and we will use it as the field on which to lay out a proven concept for producing better returns for all of the buyers and sellers in a given manufacturing chain, from Mother Earth to the consumer. We will describe the corporate structures and attitudes needed to bring about the close and trusting relationships which are essential to gaining this advantage. Along the way we will illustrate how these should enhance the power of the basic Kantian morality that each party must treat the other as ends in themselves, rather than as objects or means. For those who need to see the psychological elements of such interpersonal activity, we will introduce some simple models illustrating the power of the individual's need for recognition of their self-worth.

We believe that humankind has been given a creative flair in order to assure change, and an ability to envision a better world and the will to strive for it. Given the right motivations, it should be possible to stir these same qualities in corporations, which are, after all, a collection of humans striving within a common interest. We hope this book will serve as a kind of Rosetta stone to help the reader understand the interdependence between the corporate behavior one can usually see with considerable clarity and the personal behavior one can usually feel with considerable intensity. Helping the reader to bridge that particular gap should leave him or her with some useful new tools for getting more out of these corporate relationships. Drawing out the best that is possible between buyer and seller firms, then, is what this book is all about.

SELECTED REFERENCES

Computer Weekly, September 10, p. 12 (1987).

Runciman, G. W. *London Review of Books* (1987).

Wolf, M. *The Japanese Conspiracy*. New English Library, Sevenoaks (1984).

1
Closing the Competitive Gap—Involving the Supplier

> End the practice of awarding business on the basis of price tag alone. Purchasing must be combined with design of product, manufacturing, and sales to work with the chosen suppliers.
>
> (*Deming's Fourth Point*)

There is a gradual awareness of the growing importance of the effective, well-integrated, supplier in the struggle for industrial competitiveness. But much of it is still an intellectual awareness, little of it is a real change in orientation, and only a few firms are actually behaving differently. This is disturbing, given the increasing dependence on supplier cooperation (not just supplier "qualification") by companies with advanced manufacturing technologies and information systems. There are a number of reasons for this, including the forlorn hope, because market share is still lost, that technological and product innovation alone will solve the problem—hence GM's big spend on robotization. Back in 1983, the *Wall Street Journal* described the "new management climate" brought by the Japanese to the USA industrial scene as:

1 obsession with quality,
2 a feeling among employees that they are all part of one team,
3 the use of scientific methods to improve processes.

Numbers 1 and 3 must include the supplier, because better quality and improved processes do not just magically begin at the receiving dock.

However, what underlies our tardiness in adopting this new managerial climate? One of the most important reasons is given in an excellent book by Hayes and Wheelwright, called *Restoring our Competitive Edge—Competing through Manufacturing* (1984). Basically, they say that the West must stop looking at manufacturing as a net cost to the company, which is subject to continuous trimming; but instead must use its manufacturing operation as a "competitive weapon", as a source of competitive advantage, which keeps the business at the forefront of attractiveness to the consumer. This thinking and positioning will significantly contribute to long-term success. And they give very valid comparisons with Germany and Japan, against which Britain and the USA do quite badly. (Hayes and Wheelwright follow a line of distinguished thinkers about competitive manufacturing which includes Deming, Myron Tribus, Abernathy, Wickham, Skinner and, with a delightful style of writing, Frank Price. References to all of these are given at the end of this chapter.)

COMPETING THROUGH MANUFACTURING

The Japanese have enticed away consumers because they have offered better quality and more innovative products in the right quantities at competitive prices—excluding the minority who were dumping. Manufacturing technology *and* philosophy played a vital role in their overall business plans, revolving around the principle of "continuous improvement." Some of the continental Europeans have done the same. German companies in particular take real pride throughout their organizations in well-engineered, well-designed products. France runs a highly innovative, nationalized telecommunications service. Sweden, Italy and Spain are all increasing their competitiveness in manufactured products at a striking rate, leaving the USA somewhere behind, and Britain floundering. One reason for Britain and the USA struggling, according to Hayes and Wheelwright, is their management approach, which emphasizes rational analysis and conceptual strategizing at the expense of the management really participating in the work; short-term results at the expense of long-term success; and the management of marketing and finance at the expense of operational demands. A more overarching reason, we believe, is that both these countries emphasize individual competitiveness coupled with a demand for solutions which are tangible, immediate and preferably absolutely quantifiable, rather than the quest for excellence with all the unknowns, intangibles and controlled experimentation that that involves. This has consequences for the way we run our companies, and certainly contributed to the fact that in the last decade the USA has lost 50% of the world-wide share of its high volume, high technology, marketplace.

COMPETING THROUGH COOPERATING

Surveys in 1975 by Professors George Cabot Lodge and William F. Martin of Stanford University proved remarkably prescient. They indicated that while more than two-thirds of business executives preferred traditional American ideology, many "sense its replacement by a new set of value definitions based on communitarianism principles . . . seventy-two percent thought new values would dominate in 1985!" (Silk and Vogel, 1976).

Traditional American ideology is defined by the ruling ideas of: individualism, property rights, competition, the limited state, scientific specialization and fragmentation. Communitarianism is the idea of individual identity with the community, the right of its members to survival, income, health and other basic needs; conserving the use of property in the light of community interests; the state and society as planning agency and arbitrator; and holism, *which stresses interdependence*, replacing specialism and fragmentation.

In the business world, this suggested that by 1985 the true meaning of a business *fraternity* (collaboration, as expressed by Hayes and Wheelwright) would reemerge. This did not happen as a general rule, mainly because organizations were still being led according to absolute precepts of survival of the fittest, and the encouragement of the macho image. While the family analogy, so popular in Japan, may not be appropriate in the West, fraternity is. In the case of buying and selling, however, we *can* choose our "relations". The most important criteria for choosing will be those indicating which relations (suppliers) will help us achieve prosperity through satisfying consumers by addressing their real human needs in the most cost-effective way.

The successful companies are also those who gather around them a cluster of dealers, distributors and suppliers who seem to be sympathetic to this aim and are successful in contributing to it. The most successful are those who seem to work as a fraternity, collaborate on joint ventures and consciously serve consumer needs right from the supplier stage.

Hayes and Wheelwright refer to this as the "productive confederation," and also include customers and competitors. They assert that American manufacturers, in their drive for improving efficiency, overlooked the need to understand the productive dynamics of this confederation, and so fell behind the competition—who were prepared to face the complexity of these relationship issues in order to achieve long-term productivity.

Our focus is on what Rosabeth Moss Kanter in *The Change Masters* calls the "Fifth Constituency," i.e. bringing suppliers as the last link into the chain of constituencies the firm has to consider in its strategic development (see Chapter 6). It is what Motorola are doing in their new "partnership" approach. Tektronix Inc., the $1.3 billion, Oregon-based world leader in oscilloscope technology, published their 1986 annual report with a very clear emphasis on the importance of supplier relationships under the heading "Purchasing Excellence" (see below). And Austin Rover in England in 1987 began a whole program of creating preferred supplier relationships; although we have serious reservations over the authoritarian approach. Xerox and Honeywell, of course, are leaders in this field, while IBM, Ford and Chrysler, both in the USA and Europe, also progress steadily—and now ICL UK is doing some tremendous things out of its concept of "World Class Manufacturing".

PURCHASING EXCELLENCE

Material can account for 80% of a product's cost. So doing a better job of procurement can have a large payoff. We are on a worldwide search for better, lower-cost parts, and plan to get them by working with only the best vendors.

We have somehow, over the years, amassed a redundancy-laden list of 2224 vendors: that would come to about one for every 8 employees. Our goal is to reduce that number of vendors by over two-thirds by October, then by another one-half in the next year.

Our suppliers are good ones, but we just have too many. Such relationships are much like friendships; there is a limit to the number you can truly cultivate.

Our Purchasing Excellence goal is highest-quality components, lowest total cost. To reach it will require global materials sourcing, using worldwide benchmarks to verify we have the best price and quality, and working with key suppliers earlier in our products' design cycles, a partner-like relationship. In such "partnerships", suppliers typically participate with the customer in joint projects, and suggest ways the company can save, such as use of generic rather than custom parts.

For the vendors we select, benefits include exclusive supply contracts, larger orders, without the need to quote each year, and being able to share the reputation of our successful company.

The whole concept of marketing now needs to be reexamined because, of all the strategies we encounter in the newly competitive companies, sales promotion and advertising are the least prominent. In fact, one of the most successful and admired companies in Britain, The Body Shop, led by the remarkable Anita Roddick, had no budget for advertising and promotion. The really important concern is that of understanding and serving real end-user needs with the best quality goods or services, and those who do that best are gaining competitive advantage. So far as quality goes, processing the product or source are key. Thus, as Hayes and Wheelwright point out, manufacturing is central to gaining competitive advantage; for which task, establishing supplier relationships is the third of what they term the four Critical Activities. The simple diagram in Figure 1.1, which is adapted from one that Deming drew up

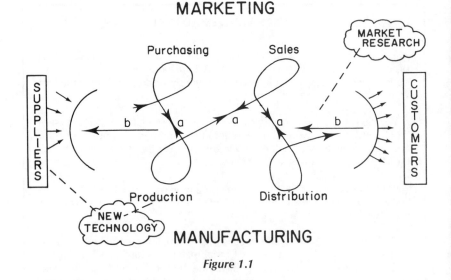

Figure 1.1

in 1950 to counter the conventional organization charts, shows the real relationship between supplying and buying companies. The relationship is characterized by a chain of internal buyer–seller interactions (a) linking the primary suppliers with the ultimate consumers. The feedback loop (b), which is the basis of capturing customers' evolving needs, provides information, not just for the processing and distribution chain; but also for the suppliers.

So it can be seen how, in reality, purchasing falls into the marketing function, because satisfaction of customer needs demands a resonance between the marketing people who identify these needs and the buyers who identify the best resources to meet them. Just as buyers and suppliers are recognizing the common ground between their companies, so buyers and their own firm's marketers must agree their common ground and optimize their relationship *internally* to satisfy the real interests of the final consumer.

A wise man once said "You had better be interested in tomorrow because that is where you will spend the rest of your life." The business of buying and selling within industries seems clearly to be experiencing a major upheaval as the complexity and velocity of events becomes even greater, and the need to look at the future more urgent. This results primarily from consumers' rapidly growing expression of their individual needs, which they demand more and more to be met individually. Naisbitt (1984) asks "Do you remember when telephones were black, bathtubs were white and checkbooks were green?" It is at once more difficult, but ever more necessary, for the production elements of industry to keep in touch with those rapidly changing demands of the consumer, and so keep their eye firmly on tomorrow. However, the emphasis on specialization and segmentation of most of our organizations causes an inward focus, which tends to obscure the consumer's need. This can leave a firm trying very hard to satisfy yesterday's desires.

It appears that the purchasing function within industry is uniquely poised to overcome such obstacles. Starting with the assembler of the final product—the last step in the manufacturing chain—it should be possible to send the necessary parameters of the consumer's needs upstream to each preceding component supplier in a way which raises the likelihood of their being more fully met in the end. The production function in the final manufacturing stage (including its purchasing activity) is closer to the customer than any production function in the rest of the chain. It is here that the consumer's needs must be most fully recognized. It is here that the flavor and the fact of the consumer's wishes enters the pipeline, to be transmitted upstream to all who need to know. It is here that the decisions between that final assembler's purchasing function and their key suppliers must be most accurately based on the consumer's true needs, and here that instructions based on those needs must be most faithfully transmitted upstream. We will present (Chapter 6) a vehicle for doing just this.

Each prior level of component or raw material production must find a way to receive and pass on to their sub-suppliers the pertinent elements of the consumers' demands which can be impacted by *any* earlier levels of manufacturing. To fail to pass along the parameters of any important consumer need, simply because it does not affect that stage of production, is to let the organization down by leaving a gap in the information chain which could make their product less likely to be the one chosen by that consumer. Again, we will present a strategy designed to minimize this risk. It will be coupled with a strategy for identifying those suppliers who are seen as absolutely best for your needs, for giving and expecting preferential treatment, and for assuring that the true will of the company enjoys a healthy chance of being executed as conceived.

The effective supplier relationship can assume many forms, but there are several elements which absolutely must be present if the relationship is to thrive and to spin off benefits for both parties:

- A trust that both parties will do what they have said they will do.
- A willingness to risk becoming vulnerable to the other party, supported by a firm belief that the other party will not take unfair advantage of that vulnerability.
- A sensitivity to each other's needs, and an active dedication to seeing that both parties' needs are met so far as that relationship can meet them.
- A high level of clear and candid communication which leaves neither party in doubt about the feelings of the other towards the relationship and the understandings within that relationship.

The pay-off from working on the relationship comes from reaching across the buyer–seller gap, thus making it possible to utilize the experience, innovation and efficiencies which are available within the collective talents of all buying and selling firms in a given production chain. This is where the creative and fulfilling opportunities are found in the search for ways to reduce the accumulation of cost, improve product quality or product features, and achieve the exceptionally effective communications essential for minimizing the inherent inefficiencies between two complex organizations. This associative relationship makes it dramatically more likely that firms in the production chain will manage to make their optimum contribution to influencing the ultimate user to buy the product or service which feeds everyone in that particular production chain. This is true even when that contribution generates a benefit useful only to firms one or more steps removed from the originator. Each buyer has this responsibility to raise the consciousness of their suppliers, who will then be inclined to raise the consciousness of each preceding supplier—all the way back to Mother Earth.

It is in this phenomenon that all of the factors previously mentioned, which are known to influence human behavior, come together to present an exceptional opportunity for the far-sighted buyer to influence other organizations to the long-term benefit of their own.

This is one of those tides in history to which Shakespeare was referring when he spoke about the "tide in the affairs of men which, taken at the flood, leads on to fortune." Competitive manufacturers, who can both recognize and realize the powerful competitive edge available to them through an associative form of relationship with their key suppliers, will most certainly improve their chances of finding fortune in the extremely demanding world market we have now entered. It is a journey into the world of these relationships upon which you embarked when you stepped into the pages of this book.

The first step of this journey is to understand ourselves at work, and to understand the organizations which provide the environment which conditions so much of what we do. Because at this time we are living with the results of unsatisfactory relationships in the past at *all* levels we need to examine these and understand how they have provided such a difficult environment for so many organizations to work in today.

SELECTED REFERENCES

Abernathy, W. J. *The Productivity Dilemma*. Johns Hopkins Press, Baltimore (1978).

Deming, W. E. *Out of the Crisis*. MIT Center for Advanced Engineering Study, Cambridge, Mass. (1988).

Hayes, R. and Wheelwright, S. *Restoring our Competitive Edge— Competing through Manufacturing*. John Wiley, New York (1984).

Kanter, R. M. *The Change Masters*. Counterpoint, London (1985).

Naisbitt, J. *Megatrends*. Futura, London (1984).

Price, F. *Right First Time*. Gower, London (1984).

Silk, L. and Vogel, D. *Ethics nad Profits*. Simon & Schuster, New York (1976).

Skinner, W. *Manufacturing in the Corporate Strategy*. John Wiley, New York (1978).

Tektronix, Inc. *1986 Annual Report*, Portland, Oregon (1987).

Tribus, M. *Deming's Way*. American Productivity Center, Productivity Brief No. 33, Houston (1984).

2
Why the Adversarial Approach no Longer Works (if it Ever Did!)

The more high technology around us, the more the need for human touch.

(Naisbitt, 1984)

Corporations can no longer leave out consideration of their major suppliers' positioning from their competitive strategy. Yet many still do, and so long as this strategy is not thought through, the less likely is an organization to be truly competitive. Even when the nature of the work does not warrant a close relationship, it is still worth reflecting consciously on what this relationship should be and what, therefore, it will add to your competitive edge. In any event, it is clear that no matter how short-term and price-sensitive the situation may be, the confrontational style has become least effective. In this chapter we will examine why, looking at it from the most basic level of human needs.

It is a general human condition that people everywhere tend to pursue their own needs and interests first. Consequently when someone comes along actually attending to the needs of others, seemingly at the expense of their own, we see them as odd and occasionally, more charitably, as saintly. Mother

Theresa of Calcutta is famous because she behaves in a way that is so clearly different from the rest of us. In some cases, these altruistic behaviors lead us to distrust the do-gooders, and to look for the hidden motives. In other cases the observers are genuinely puzzled by this "unprofitable" activity; in particular those who get a real kick out of accumulating a lot of material wealth. (Ivan Boesky would come into this category— as an extreme example.)

It is particularly clear in business dealings between firms that self-interest (whatever that means) is a prime motive for doing most things. None of us today will live long enough to change that, even if we felt it helpful so to do. It is far more useful to accept self-interest as an initial force shaping the actions on both sides of any important relationship, and to proceed to find ways to work with it.

The best way of working with this self-interest is first to understand it. Here is a model which explains what we mean by self-interest, and how it needs to be taken into account in interpersonal relationships. It resulted from research carried out by Clayton Alderfer between 1968 and 1974. He identified three categories of needs, each one leading to the next as it was satisfied. This is a direct development from Maslow's original hierarchy of needs, which proved such a useful device for understanding how people are motivated, but minus the hierarchical implications of being better as you progressed upwards.

Thus, everyone tries to satisfy the particular need which is most pressing at that time, regardless of its type. That is in their self-interest, and it means that satisfying Existence Needs, such as a house purchase, is no less worthy than striving towards such Growth Needs as creativity and self-fulfilment. What is important, however, is to know by which need the buyer or the seller is feeling pressed if you wish to influence them effectively. Our experience strongly suggests that most suppliers today are looking for Relatedness Needs satisfaction in their interactions with buying organizations; but are being treated as if Existence Needs satisfaction was their only goal.

The implications of this are addressed by another important aspect of Alderfer's theory: that two needs can operate simultaneously. So if a particular path towards satisfaction of a need

Table 2.1   Alderfer's categories of needs

Type 1	Type 2	Type 3
Existence Needs	Relatedness Needs	Growth Needs
All forms of psychological and natural desires, including money	Relationships with people and their need for recognition of worth or self-esteem	The desire to be creative and to achieve full potential
As Type 1 needs are met, we begin looking to meet Type 2 needs	As Type 2 needs are met, we begin looking to meet Type 3 needs	

is blocked, the individual will both persist along that path and, at the same time, regress towards more easily satisfied needs. Thus, if suppliers are being treated as though the only reason they wish to interact is because they want more money (Type 1 Need) *then, in fact, that is how they will behave on the surface.* (Note that Deming maintains "your suppliers are what you make them".) But at the same time they will be trying to give out messages of a different sort, mainly that they actually need a more meaningful relationship (Type 2 Need). This mixed message will be treated in a way the buyer will be most comfortable with (the easiest option) and that will usually be on the money basis (Type 1 Need). Hence the relationship will be characterized by a series of short-term interactions and will not have a developmental quality.

It seems fair to conclude that you, the reader, also have Relatedness Needs, which are being met at least partly by your organization. If so, the rules and customs of your company very much shape your individual behavior when representing your firm in business dealings—as does the particular concept of morality which you bring to the job. This chemistry of influences on individual human beings as they strive to do what they perceive to be best for their employers, must be made visible before decisions about effective relationships can be consciously entered into. These implicit influences have always been there; it is now time to use them explicitly for your own and your firm's advantage. If a problem well stated is a problem half-solved, we shall travel some distance towards the best solutions.

BUSINESS DEALINGS—HOW THESE AFFECT THE WAY WE WORK

It happens that the business of buying and selling frequently places our assessment of self-worth under assault. In the days of simple barter before money came into use as a unit of measure for trade, people hoped to use the product of their day's effort to secure a commodity which took the other party at least a day's effort to produce. It is easy to picture the damage to one's assessment of self-worth when the other party demands a product requiring two days of your own labor in exchange for a product requiring only one day of theirs—even if they do have a monopoly. A few heads were no doubt split by stone axes over this very point!

It is this challenge to individual or corporate self-worth which tends to inject adversarial conditions into so much of the negotiating done by Western individuals and Western companies. This probably added a competitive edge to the spirit of enterprise, which worked well enough during the Mercantile Age when new market horizons were being discovered every day. It continued to be satisfactory through the Industrial Revolution when new manufacturing processes, developed mostly in the Western countries, were spewing out unprecedented quantities of goods with fewer and fewer hours of anyone's labor in them. It also happened that this increased supply coincided with a relatively undemanding consumer population, which persisted until quite recently, and whose tastes were dictated more by the narrow choice available than by their actual preferences.

Today, however, we are in the process of moving from the Industrial Age to the Information Age and face a more sophisticated and demanding consumer population. This development, combined with the greater choice now available and the growing possibility of transporting all goods to and from all markets efficiently, causing the world market to function more like one giant bazaar, has worked against the West, where the expansion of overseas markets has now been replaced by an expansion of overseas competition. It is time to assess what lessons we have learned from this about competition, consumers and supplier relations, particularly regarding quality and price, as it is no longer the case that the product can be priced according solely to the cost of making it.

To provide just one example, consider the recent history of the US auto industry. From the Model T to the Mustang (introduced as a 1965 model), US car and truck makers competed almost exclusively with each other in the largest auto market in the world. Conventional wisdom in Detroit held it unthinkable that imports would ever take as much as 10% of the domestic market. The only import causing any serious concern was the Volkswagen Beetle, which was dismissed as serving an insignificant and unattractive market niche. Toyota's first postwar venture into the US from 1959 to 1964 had been a total disaster because of the poor quality and design of the vehicles for continuous high speed travel. Toyota then retreated to its own shores, much chastened by its encounter with the manufacturing and marketing muscle of America's Big Four (American Motors was then still one of the mainstream US auto makers). By the year the Mustang was introduced in 1964, auto imports from all countries took only 6.1% of the US market, and Japan's share had risen to only a minuscule three-tenths of one percent. So what happened to cause Japan to have increased its share of the market by over 7000%, taking nearly 70% of the total exports to the USA? (Europe suffered the same import shock; although not to the same extent). Basically this resulted from a difference in philosophy about managing organizations, a philosophy that was so successful that by February 1983 the USA and the European Economic Community had felt constrained to negotiate a series of VER ("voluntary export restraint") agreements with Japan over automobiles, VCRs, several categories of consumer electronics, and numerically controlled machine tools.

RELATIONSHIPS, PRICE AND QUALITY

During the 1950s and the 1960s, any inefficiencies between the US car makers and their suppliers could be passed along in the price of the vehicle because all builders shared pretty much the same suppliers and all would incur pretty much the same increase. And they all tended to use basically the same adversarial approach with their suppliers, providing very little feeling of any relationship beyond each contract to do business for the current model year. It was a large and classic example of the level playing field, which business people long for, and these increases were passed on to the consumer with no real corresponding quality improvement in the product. A parallel interaction occurred in the British car industry, except that, to add insult to injury, for the consumer, reliability also declined noticeably.

This adversarial tendency between the auto makers and their suppliers resulted in a great deal of management energy being spent on both sides in search of ways to capture some of the other party's margin. There were also sporadic and sometimes successful attempts to cooperate in true reduction of costs such as transit damage, scrap and rework expense. But for the most part, the hammer came down on price, price, price— meaning the selling price of the supplier—and they too often responded, understandably, by cutting costs at the expense of quality.

The management styles of the four firms were somewhat different from each other, but not dramatically. All were unionized largely by the United Auto Workers, as were a great many of their larger suppliers. The management–union relationship was almost totally adversarial at all levels, with the burning question every three years being *which* of the auto makers would be that round's strike target. Couple this with the lack of an outside constraint, and it is not difficult to see how US auto industry wages and salaries got significantly out of line with the other basic industries.

In the end, of course, it is the actual consumer who must pay for everything which happens, from Mother Earth to themselves; in this case from the extraction of iron ore, silicon, bauxite, etc., through the melting, smelting, forging, stamping, machining and sub-assembly to the final assembly and delivery of the vehicle to the dealer's showroom. And the inefficient, adversarial, condition mentioned earlier existed more or less at every one of the buy–sell interfaces along the way. We are, after all, largely a product of our Western frontier history, which rewards rugged individualism. We tend to think "I'm all right, Jack, I've got *my* six-gun. If you've got yours, it will be a fair fight." With management, labor and suppliers fighting a three-way battle to cut the pie more in their own favor, it is not hard to see how they somewhat lost sight of their collective need to be competitive in front of the person who would decide whether to feed all or none of them—the vehicle buyer, the ultimate consumer. This same sorry history repeated itself to one degree or another in the steel industry, textiles and in the brown and white goods industries in both Europe and the USA.

The Japanese, of course, are products of a very different history, which rewards cooperation and mutual support. They have a saying "It is the nail whose head stands up which gets pounded down." Consequently they work hard at identifying those with whom they have a common interest (such as being collectively competitive in front of the ultimate consumer) and to find ways to pursue that common interest to the mutual benefit of both. Couple this "family" tendency with the manufacturing quality lessons they have embraced from W. Edwards Deming, beginning in the 1950s, plus the longer-term Oriental view of management and market strategy, and their emergence on the US and European scene with attractive, high-quality, inexpensive cars in the late 1960s seems, in retrospect, almost preordained.

As the US car makers began to feel heat from this new player in the market, they found it increasingly difficult to base their product pricing on their accumulated costs, because the new player was beginning to set the market price by offering that ultimate consumer a viable alternative. So, not only were US makers losing volume, they also lost margin.

The Japanese had done their homework on the US market rather well, by and large. They could see that the car buyers yearned for a more reliable vehicle with better "fit and finish"—in other words, more for your money. They seldom competed solely on price, even though they started with lower costs for labor and purchased components. Since then, although their labor costs have moved inexorably closer to those in the USA, their cost of purchased components has continued to seem almost unapproachable by our standards. This is largely because manufacturer and supplier have worked in concert on upgrading quality and reducing costs.

With purchased components and materials representing 60–80% of the manufactured cost of most automobiles and trucks, any excessive inefficiencies between US car makers and their suppliers will only serve to reduce margins all along the manufacturing chain, as they can no longer be passed along so easily to the marketplace. Left to its own devices, this narrowing of margins will only force people out of business in the manufacturing chain and further weaken the infrastructure of the entire industry.

Importing lower-cost foreign components and materials is not a viable long-term solution as it involves *adding* cost (transportation, damage, inflexibility to market changes) to the accumulation of cost from Mother Earth to the consumer. Unfortunately for the US economy, and for the British car industry in particular, off-shore sourcing, primarily to Far East suppliers, has been a growing phenomenon. In Britain especially, this has been happening largely because the relationship between car builder and component supplier has been such that joint development as an acceptable way of working has not been widely possible—largely due to an atmosphere of hostility and mistrust.

PEOPLE AND PRODUCTION

As you read this, the above scenario is repeating itself all too often in the Western industrialized countries. As the developing nations acquire efficient Western product and manufacturing process technology—which is offered for sale to them—and harness it with inherently lower labor costs, their ability to knock Western manufacturers from the catbird seat, even in Western markets, grows daily.

We in the Western world profess belief in the long-term benefits of the free market, so we are not about to curtail the sale of productivity-improving equipment to Korea, Taiwan, Singapore and the other developing nations. And we are not very anxious to hold back wages to match the generally lower rates paid in those countries, although "give-backs" may be necessary in the extreme cases. So this could become a mega-scale reenactment of the Perils of Pauline, as she lies tied to the railroad track with the train thundering toward her, unless the West can find ways to untie their workers and free their remarkable creative talents to become more competitive at the consumer level. But unless the employees feel their needs being met, why should they expend energy contributing to the firm's ultimate success?

The following excerpts from an interview with Ross Perot published in the English *Business* magazine in February 1987 illustrate this point. *Business* indicated that Mr Perot was paid $700,000,000 by General Motors for his Class E shares largely to silence his repeated assertions that cars are built by people, not robots, and that the firm's problems stem more from management's treatment of the people who build those cars (and their components) than from any other single factor.

INTERVIEW WITH ROSS PEROT

QUESTION: Is it true that the American worker can no longer compete with Asians and West Europeans?

ANSWER: The problem is not with the American working person. The people who work in our factories are as good as anybody in the world. The problem is the lack of leadership and direction.
. . . a lot of what they do is inefficient because of bad planning, bad layout and bad design. That comes from the top of the organization.

QUESTION: Why did GM spend millions to acquire British Lotus . . . ?

ANSWER: I asked that very question. I said, "What are we buying here?" and they said, "[Lotus engineers] were terribly creative." I said "[GM] has thousands of engineers and you are saying that the Lotus few are more creative than ours?" They said, "[The Lotus] engineers work in an entirely different environment." I said "Why don't we keep the money and change the environment and unleash the potential of thousands of our engineers?" That's the challenge—changing the environment.

QUESTION: What about the new environment reforms hinted at in the "plant of the future"—GM's Saturn operation in Tennessee?

ANSWER: The greatest impact of Saturn is the personnel philosophy which didn't cost anything to implement. You could dramatically improve the company by implementing the Saturn philosophy across GM even now. . . .

The Saturn philosophy is treating people with dignity—treating people like human beings, making them a part of the team, listening to their suggestions and ideas.

During the same month that *Business* published the above article, *Business Week* magazine in the USA authorized a poll of US consumers, 40% of whom stated that they felt Ross Perot was right in his criticism of the way GM was being run, while only 19% supported Roger Smith. The article further reports that GM's break-even point has gone up 30% since 1981 in spite of a massive $40 billion capital spending program in the 80s to automate and modernize its manufacturing operations. At Buick City in Flint, Michigan, the highly publicized $400 million refurbishing with robot welders, electronically guided material carts and the latest high technology process equipment resulted in one of the slowest start-ups of any auto plant on record. The Buick City's start-up agony was apparently prolonged by GM's "archaic management style." One officer of the United Auto Workers local chapter stated that "GM is way overloaded with supervision, and they won't listen to people on the floor."

Part of the human process problem is lack of communication, and there is stunning evidence that listening to the people on the shop floor can pay handsome dividends, even in the USA, even in the auto industry, even in a UAW plant formerly operated in the traditional GM manner. In Fremont, California, in 1984, GM and Toyota jointly reopened an auto assembly plant, which GM had closed two years before, largely because it was one of the poorest-performing operations in the company. It has been managed since its reopening with much of the original workforce, but in the Toyota manner, with flexible work roles and significant worker control over operations. The factory is now about 50% more efficient than it had been, and roughly 40% more efficient than a currently operating, otherwise-comparable, GM plant, according to a study by the Massachusetts Institute of Technology.

And if the managers of GM do not listen very well to the workers in their own plants, they are probably even less likely to listen to their suppliers and the workers of their suppliers. While GM has poured billions of dollars into its own facilities, Ford and Chrysler have made even wider use of outside suppliers by attempting to concentrate their purchases from those who have the very best track records in quality, cost reduction and innovation. They are then able to move production from their own facilities to those selected suppliers when and where it becomes clear that there is a long-term competitive advantage in cost or quality or specialized expertise. The same approach is used by the best European manufacturers. They are all proving that mutual benefits occur when customer firms go beyond treating suppliers as merely additional units of production, and begin attending consciously to their needs in order to achieve the right relationship.

We are not here indulging in the popular pastime of bashing GM because they are everyone's popular whipping-boy. We are using them as the archetypal, highly bureaucratized, giant organization, which so often suffers because it has forgotten how to incorporate *relationship thinking* into its *corporate planning*. British Telecom would have been an appropriate alternative example at this time, given their quality and morale problems of 1987. The world needs companies like GM and British Telecom to succeed because they affect the lives of millions of people; but so long as they impose structural solutions to human *process* problems, they will not be able to resist the erosion of their effectiveness. But perhaps all that will change now. General Motors have at last taken Deming's total quality message seriously, and have demonstrated this by putting the remarkable Bill Scherkenbach in charge of quality in the Buick Oldsmobile Cadillac (BOC) Division. Nevertheless, they will still have to reduce in size first to satisfy their shareholders, which may not be the best start.

So, in summary, one of the largest remaining, largely untapped, opportunities for becoming competitive through the quality approach and subsequent cost (not simply price) reduction lies at the interfaces between the buyers and sellers up and down each production chain. Suppliers tend to find a special market niche and develop superior skills and efficiencies in order to thrive in that niche. In so doing, they become dependent on an effective two-way relationship with their buying organizations, and if this sense of dependence becomes a state of anxiety and anger, because the relationship is felt to be one-sided, it is a waste of synergy. It is the process for unlocking this very substantial potential for benefiting everyone in that production chain which is the special message of this book.

SELECTED REFERENCES

Alderfer, C. P. *Existence, Relatedness and Growth: Human Needs in Organizational Settings*. The Free Press, New York (1972).
Business Week, February (1987).
Inman, B. "The Wisdom of H. Ross Perot," *Business*, February, pp. 90–91 (1987).
Naisbitt, J. *Megatrends*. Futura, London (1984).

3
Buyer–Seller Interdependence

Manufacturers can no longer view suppliers simply as a source for components they do not want to make themselves.

(Burt and Soukup, 1985)

Given the earlier premise that people everywhere share a primal drive as individuals to attend first and foremost to their own needs, it follows that the best way to influence people will necessitate understanding those needs in some way.

The American Indians say "If you would understand the other brave, walk a mile in his moccasins." It is reasonably easy to recognize that a person's ability to influence or persuade you to do something is almost totally dependent on your perception of their willingness to help you meet *your* needs. It is slightly more difficult—but a moment of absolute truth—to recognize that precisely the opposite is also true. Your ability to persuade another person to do something you want them to do is almost entirely dependent on *their* perception of *your* willingness to help them meet *their* needs. This simple but profound insight can help you become much more successful at influencing others.

INTERDEPENDENCE

Confucius taught in 500 BC that there were five important interdependencies in life: father/son, older brother/younger

28

brother, ruler/subject, friend/friend and husband/wife. He taught that proper ethical behavior required that these interdependencies should be given special treatment in order to improve the quality of life. Specifically, he urged that both parties concentrate on enlarging the benefits of the interdependency, rather than each attempting to enlarge their own share of said benefit. In other words, make more pie rather than attempt to cut the pie more in your own favor. By so doing, he reasoned, you would be working together to create additional pie, and you would share in the happy result when more pie was ultimately available for both of you. It may seem almost too simple to accept, but this fundamental tenet of human nature determines much of our reaction to the people around us, whether they be friend, spouse, offspring, boss, or business associate.

While writing on business ethics, Peter Drucker (1982) addressed this very point when he said

> Right behavior—which in the English translation of Confucian ethics is usually called "sincerity"—is that individual behavior which is truly appropriate to the specific relationship of mutual dependence because it optimizes benefits for both parties. Other behavior is "insincere" and therefore wrong behavior and unethical. It creates dissonance instead of harmony, exploitation instead of benefits, manipulation instead of trust.

Nowhere is the corporate corollary of this basic behavioral tenet more apparent than in the relationship between customer and supplier businesses.

> *Nowhere in business is there greater potential for benefiting from such interdependency than between customer firms and their suppliers. This is the largest remaining frontier for gaining competitive advantage—and nowhere has such a frontier been more neglected.*

Right now, even as quality standards and rates of technological change demand greater cooperation, only a very few firms are adopting strategies designed to develop a truly interdependent relationship with their key suppliers. One reason is that most customer firms simply have not thought deeply about relationships before and, having not thought about them, they need to start at square one if now they want to change.

Only when the individuals representing each firm perceive the other firm as being interested in helping meet their needs can the relationship prosper. If at any time, one of the parties perceives a diminishing interest by the other in seeing that the first party's needs are met, that relationship begins to sour rapidly. The ultimate failure in such a relationship occurs when the two must meet in court and ask a third party to decide whose needs shall be met and to what extent.

To examine how, instead, any two parties can cause their relationship to grow stronger and to become more beneficial to both parties is the major objective of this book. We will show you how to move any relationship between two firms upward toward what we call the "associative" level, where the companies jointly explore the future and will even sacrifice some degree of their own short-term interest in order to help the other meet an even larger need. In that direction lies a happier future with ample rewards for all.

In the other direction, characterized by adversarial attitudes, lie more of the wasted opportunities and resources that have characterized these last stages of our Western industrial society. This, combined with unhelpful economic policies, can only bring further decline in the wealth-producing sectors. Other countries, whose cultures allow them to understand more clearly the interdependent relationship, will continue to attract consumers to buy their products. These imports feed the overseas manufacturing chains by using our consumer's wealth—instead of that wealth being used to feed local industry—and a large share of the blame must be attributed to the fact that we are not optimizing the buyer–seller relationship.

THE NEGOTIATING RELATIONSHIP

Self-Perception versus Self-Deception

First, let us get away from all the slogans and catchphrases, which are creeping into negotiation just as they did into selling, and look at the real meaning of buyer–supplier relationships.

These are characterized by the way they negotiate, which is often very different from the way they say they negotiate!

Much has been written about negotiation—a most seductive topic—and a lot is bunkum. It has been confused with bazaar haggling, conflict resolution and even straightforward selling. Myths have been fed, clever short-term tricks praised and obsolete practices held up as contemporary wisdom. In fact, negotiating has been debased by far too much "win–lose" advice by so-called experienced experts and games-playing theorists.

So, thank goodness for Fisher and Ury's (1983) *Getting to Yes*, which makes up for many of these misleading publications, and which contains sound practical advice, as well as some clear moral imperatives, emphasizing as it does "principled negotiation." The fact that it is such a best-seller is clear evidence that most negotiators do have an intuitive understanding of what it really is all about. You cannot fool a practical negotiator even some of the time; although you can frustrate them a lot of the time.

The way an organization treats its suppliers is very often an indicator of where it is in terms of its own development and values. The truism that subordinates behave as their superiors do can be extended beyond corporate boundaries, i.e. the way an organization behaves internally often governs the nature of its buying relationships. So, although this chapter concentrates on negotiation, it is not intended just for purchasing negotiators. It also has a powerful message for those senior executives who manage any of the touch-points of the buyer–supplier interface, such as product engineering, manufacturing and quality control. These are the people in charge of the image that the organization has in the marketplace. They consciously or otherwise shape the buying culture and can make or break a developing supplier relationship. For example, how often has an organization voiced platitudes about the understanding and flexible relationship it has with its suppliers, when, in fact, the individual buyers work from an authoritarian environment which allows them very little scope for being flexible and cooperative? The answer is "many times"—and their suppliers are constantly frustrated by having to deal with a buyer who is trapped with them in a system-driven, price-reduction, relationship which has been frozen for years. The British automobile industry has been notorious for such conditions.

It is easy to understand why suppliers find this threatening as well as frustrating. We have talked to suppliers, both in Britain and in the United States, who feel a genuine grievance toward major corporations whose benevolent public attitude is belied by rigid price-driven buying policies—and all too often it is the buyer who is the meat in this sandwich, feeling very uneasy about the power wielded by their spending ability, yet limited by the fixed conditions which do not permit the obvious needs of the supplier to be met. Usually their behavior is typical of any normal person when confronted by such a contradiction: they say "No" to anything that is the slightest bit different. This also applies to the other touch-point disciplines who are trapped in this same net—with the same negative consequences. These consequences are most often uneven implementations, which diminish the potential benefits of any joint efforts, damage the relationship itself and discredit the public "good image" statements of the purchasing organization's executive, by leaving the strong impression that the customer firm really does not care whether a given supplier lives or dies.

Implementations Matter

The overwhelming objective for any negotiators worth their salt is not an agreement, but a successful implementation. Again and again, we have seen skilled negotiators walk away from negotiations because they thought that the implications of the proposed agreement had not been thought through, or because it had win–lose elements to it. And again and again, we have seen these successful negotiators persevere for hours on end because they thought that, despite all the differences, a win–win solution was feasible, because the relationship seemed right. The Japanese seem to be the archetypal examples of this relationship-exploring approach, and have infuriated many Westerners by their slow, careful, definition and development of the kind of feelings and attitudes which are required to support the business relationship.

To quote Peter Drucker (*Wall Street Journal*, July 18, 1985) again

The Japanese way [of conducting business] may indeed not be particularly difficult. But it is quite different. The first difference— and the one most Westerners find hardest to grasp—is that you don't "do" business in Japan. Business is not an "activity"; it is a "commitment." The purchasing agent orders goods, to be sure. But first he commits himself to a supplier, and to a relationship that is presumed to be permanent or at least long-lasting. And until the newcomer—whether Japanese or foreign—proves itself committed in turn, the purchasing agent will not buy its wares no matter how good their quality or how cheap their price.

Negotiation, the Tip of the Iceberg

On the surface, the negotiator bargains, explores, stands firm and works intensely with the other party, seemingly giving all the attention to talking, persuading and arguing. But beneath the surface the equally important activities of creating the conditions for a successful negotiation and implementation are also taking place. This is the "rest of the iceberg," and it is misleading to try to understand any negotiating situation without considering its context.

We will examine this; then look at some of the best practices which produce the most effective relationships; and finally offer some ideas on how buyers can best meet the future in these terms. But first, a brief excursion into the history of negotiation, which may help us to understand why it is so important to develop the relationship deliberately and consciously.

Negotiation: its Increasing Visibility through History

Negotiation as a phenomenon fascinates both academics and non-academics alike. In one book alone by Rubin and Brown (1975) there is a bibliography of over 800 articles and books on the subject. Why this interest? One reason is obviously the sheer number of distressing political failures in this field. From Yalta to SALT there has been a catalogue of disasters, many of which, had they occurred in a business context, would have demanded the resignation of the chief executive.

The second reason we advance as a hypothesis. Negotiation is fascinating today because many people are involved in important negotiations, which, 100 years ago, would have been the preserve and right of a chosen few. From ancient times, when Moses argued the case of the Jews, against a very powerful party indeed(!), through the late fifteenth century, when European diplomacy was established and the Treaty of Tordesillas exemplified international relations (in which Spain and Portugal agreed to divide the unexplored part of the world), to the great industrial alliances forged in the Victorian era, negotiations were conducted by "notable personages"— and then only with other "notable personages." The lower orders within the organizations merely carried out the agreements—to the letter.

Today, however, many corporations have the same relative impact as those medieval political states had, and negotiations are carried out at levels far below those at which the big states operated. That is not to say that decisions are necessarily made at these lower levels; but they are shaped there, and the individual buyer very often becomes the organization in the eyes of the supplier. So at the very least it is there that the beginnings of a working relationship are forged—or miscast. When one stops to consider the size of the investment made on the basis of some of these negotiations, the question has to be asked: just how conscious are those individual buyers of the impact of the decisions they are bringing to fruition? Concomitantly, to what extent are purchasing departments used by senior executives as barriers to an understanding of reality of their supplier situation, by their making the buyers the "nasties" with the unreasonable demands?

There is considerable evidence that far too often the buck stops, not with the senior executive, but with the buyers. This may be one reason why many purchasing negotiators have a somewhat limited view of the procurement process, and why so many suppliers feel frustrated and therefore contribute less than they might. A typical example of a real case is given below.

A supplier to a major and progressive mid-Western firm, was invited to join their Supplier Council, composed of the best firms among their preferred suppliers. At the meeting of this council he was told by senior customer management that his ideas were welcomed, and that he should bring any suggestions for product improvement or cost reduction to the appropriate buyer, who would then pursue the idea internally through the evaluation process to a decision.

Knowing of a manufacturing problem on the customer's line which was made worse by one of the parts he furnished, he set out to redesign his part in a way which would eliminate the difficulty. After considerable effort, he found a way to redesign his part which made final assembly easier and less costly. It also produced a final product with superior reliability. It would save the customer's manufacturing operation several dollars per assembly, and would add only a few cents to the cost of his component, while also eliminating a reliability problem the ultimate consumer was experiencing.

With great anticipation he laid this out for the buyer of his component, who rejected it out of hand. It seems that this buyer's performance was measured primarily on the purchased price of the component. To accept this idea would very likely diminish his apparent performance and, possibly, even his annual bonus.

Senior management would have welcomed this idea had they known about it, but the buyer not only declined to pursue it, he warned the supplier not to "go around him" in an attempt to get the idea accepted. The buyer's personal "consequences" system was not in tune with the firm's stated goals—because the system for measuring/rewarding buyer performance had not caught up with senior management's stated new policy. So trust was destroyed, and with it the kind of relationship which would have benefited both organizations.

So, what is this phenomenon known as negotiation, and why is it so demanding? Let us take another brief excursion into the past.

The word "negotiation" has its root in the Latin word *"otium"* meaning "leisure". *Neg-otium* became current as the slave population in Rome dwindled and Romans discovered they had less and less spare time. Thus they negotiated for their leisure, their pursuit of quality life. And in fact all negotiations should be a means of achieving an enhanced quality of life and work; hence the term *"win–win,"* which should mean more than just improvement (except if you happened to be a slave!). It should mean, in fact, a situation in which each issue requiring resolution has been settled in a way which meets the *needs* of both parties, even though either, or both, may have been hoping for more. So we can already see two of the conditions necessary for an effective negotiation to take place, i.e.

1 *A scarce resource or a perceived need* which creates an inter-dependence between the two parties, although some conflict over objectives.
2 *An intention on both sides* to achieve an agreement on win–win terms so that both parties can see why it is in their own interest to insure implementation of each component precisely as agreed.

The third condition is the one Roman slaves did not really possess, that of

3 *The ability to vary the terms.* This gives freedom and power to the negotiator, and should also bring responsibility. How negotiators exercise these qualities, and how the organization permits their exercise, is fundamental to effective relationships.

The important point to recognize is that a negotiation does not exist in a vacuum. It comprises internal and external relations; it has specific stages through which it moves towards agreement; and it exists within a time dimension. These are all points which have been recognized to a greater or lesser extent by most writers on the subject. However, the neglected aspect of negotiation is the developmental dimension; the fact that it is often the key phase in an evolving relationship between the two parties through which they need to pass if the relationship is to mature.

The Developing Business Relationship

When seen in this light, it becomes clear that an effective long-term business relationship between mature organizations is one which moves from straightforward selling and buying transactions to an associative one, which emphasizes long-term common interests. This transition is conducted most effectively

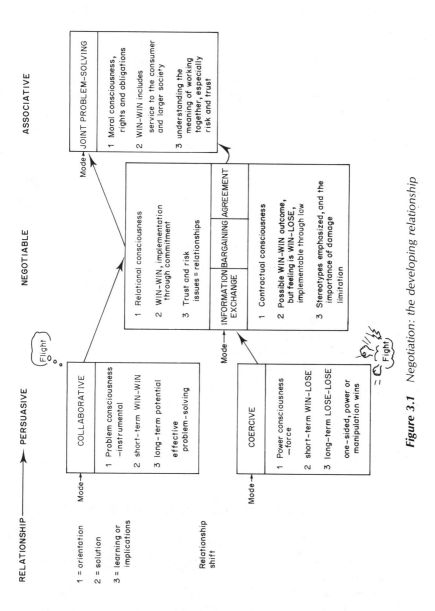

Figure 3.1 *Negotiation: the developing relationship*

through the medium of negotiation. Unfortunately, negotiation, because of its high profile, is far too often regarded as the way buyers and sellers should always relate, thus there is no opportunity for the relationship to develop. It should, however, be treated more as a *transition* phase between the other two relationships, containing qualities of each, and addressing the interests of both parties. This would explain the uncomfortable dynamics and help people deal more successfully with the characteristic tension, which so often leads to those cold, static (strictly business) interactions, which in turn lead to interminable renegotiations and a mechanistic relationship!

The tension described in the previous paragraph is only resolved if the negotiation activity is consciously guided and transformed by the negotiator into a more associative relationship along the path illustrated in Figure 3.1. Thus negotiation is the bridge used as a *rites de passage* by one party in the business relationship to lead the other across the threshold of a new relationship, a new way of working together. It is carried out in a conscious, skilled, way which can be *helped or hindered by the organization* (usually hindered!); but which can never replace the personal resources of an effective human being. This responsibility for developing the relationship is the personal challenge for all negotiators, particularly those with real power, and it is a major challenge for effective businesses in the 1980s and 1990s because we simply must come to trust each other more in Western manufacturing, if we are to cooperate well enough to sustain anything like the standards of quality and performance which make us competitive.

No Negotiation is an Island (although it may be an iceberg!)

It is now clear that conditions within the organization can prove a strait-jacket to would-be win–win negotiation: let us analyze why.

The most useful model for doing this was one put forward by Carlisle and Leary, in a 1981 publication, which first raised the concept of "Intra Negotiating Groups," i.e. those internal groups, within the negotiator's own organization, with whom

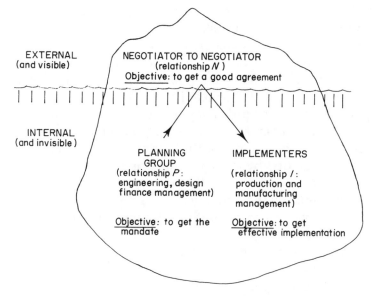

Figure 3.2   *Key negotiating relationships*

the negotiator has to deal in order to:

(a) get the mandate to negotiate effectively, such as sufficient flexibility, clear objectives, and a thorough understanding of the real issues at stake—as well as help with the planning process.
(b) influence the implementer of the agreement in their own organization to carry it out effectively.

The best way to look at this positioning is again as an iceberg (see Figure 3.2).

It is the nature of these internal relationships (P and I) that often determines the nature of the external negotiating relationship, despite the negotiators' own predilections. Time and again we have observed individual buyers whose natural instincts for leading chosen suppliers into the mutually beneficial associative relationship were frustrated by short-term internal objectives and even conflicting mandates given by their management. The result is the appearance to the supplier of a customer firm who has very little interest in helping the supplier meet their long-term needs. It follows that the supplier will offer their best ideas and best efforts elsewhere, to some other customer, who *does* seem willing to help meet those long-term needs. Because these ideas are the stuff from which real progress is made, the resulting opportunity loss to the customer firm can be enormous. That loss will be silent, unseen, unknown and sometimes deadly, as other firms with good supplier relationships pull away in the competitive race.

The specific buyer bears some responsibility for failing to attract the very best effort of this supplier; but remember that the buyer is guided by the very same principle—that is, long-term self-interest. And when the consequence to the buyer and the consequence to the employer firm are in conflict, the buyer will lower his or her aspirations to the level of Alderfer's Existence Needs and go for the price reduction.

This phenomenon in which the firm causes the conditions which damage the relationship is not sufficiently understood because organizations, and the people in them, are not sufficiently understood by the people who run them. We need to put that right, and the first step is to understand some of the human forces at work in our modern industrial world which bring about these negative conditions. We shall do this in Chapter 4.

SELECTED REFERENCES

Burt, D. N. and Soukup, W. R. "Purchasing's Role in New Product Development," *Harvard Business Review*, September–October, pp. 90–97 (1985).

Carlisle, J. A. and Leary, M. "Negotiating Groups," in C. Cooper and R. Payne (eds), *Groups at Work*. John Wiley, Chichester (1981).

Drucker, P. F. *The Changing World of the Executive*. Heinemann, London (1982).

Fisher, R. and Ury, W. *Getting to Yes*. Hutchison, London (1983).

Rubin, J. and Brown, B. *The Social Psychology of Bargaining and Negotiation*. Academic Press, New York (1975).

4
Risk and Trust—and the
Development of Relationships

We must welcome the future, remembering that soon it will be the
past; and we must respect the past, remembering that once it was all
that was humanly possible.

(George Santayana)

The last chapter made the following points:

1   The relationship between buyer and supplier that works
    best is one of acknowledged interdependence. In fact,
    ideally, all business relationships should be like this.
2   Negotiation is an essential process for developing a rela-
    tionship if used effectively. Too often, however, it is used in
    a way which freezes that relationship.
3   The most frequent cause of this freezing of the relationship
    is the attitude of the management responsible for purchas-
    ing policies and practices, i.e. those who create the reward
    systems which shape the performance of the internal nego-
    tiation groups. They seldom display a realistic understand-
    ing of the supplier's situation and consequently a real
    interest in meeting their needs. This naturally reflects itself
    in the negotiator's behavior.
4   We now need to consciously improve and develop the
    relationship between buyers and sellers.

Unfortunately, while some of the solutions are clearly emerging, based on changing the nature of the relationship itself, it is not an easy route to follow. We need to change our *thinking* about the way we work in order to allow more time for nurturing the right relationships. And we need to introduce a greater degree of openness in our dealings. In other words, allow a greater degree of *trust* and take greater *risks* with people.

Even if we accept the need to do this, however, we must be realistic about the obstacles that will bar our path. Two forces, in particular, seem to work against the widespread use of the associative approach:

1   The emphasis in the West on short-term results. This creates a formidable array of incentives to perform well (or at least to be perceived as performing well) in the short term— usually meaning no longer than the coming year, and, in some cases, the coming quarter.

The main culprits in this are impatient Western investors and the fluidity of Western equity markets, compounded by the mobility of Western executives. The personal "consequences" system, which largely determines the progress and compensation of the individual, is too often loaded with short-term rewards for short-term progress.

2   This "short-termism" is especially true for industrial buyers who are frequently measured largely, if not totally, on direct price reductions achieved in the current year.

We have seen innumerable cases where this focus has worked against the longer-term competitive vigour of the firm. As we saw in the previous chapter, a blind attention to price reduction by the buyer leaves many good ideas for *cost reduction* lying stillborn when it is seen that their benefit accrues in quality, product features, or anywhere other than direct purchase price. This constitutes a severe impediment to developing and enjoying the benefits of the long-term relationship between buying and selling firms, based on trust which is so essential to unlocking the competitive advantages we are after.

Here is a case taken from the IMP Project Group's research into industrial marketing and purchasing in Europe (Hakansson, 1982). The two paint companies referred to are both British. Unfortunately Colorex is still the more common example.

PURCHASING STRATEGY OF COLOREX

(reproduced by permission of John Wiley & Sons Ltd)

Foreign supplies are used extensively and 15 per cent of supplies come from sources outside the UK. Purchasing efficiency is the principal element of the strategy in buying; this efficiency is evaluated by comparing Colorex purchasing costs with those of other firms in the industry and also by studying buying achievements obtained against suppliers. Financial gains, through price bargaining, is the main evidence used in considering buying efficiency; such "gains" are to be found in the following tactics with suppliers:

1 Buying at prices below those quoted on supplier's list prices.
2 Paying accounts later than specified by suppliers.
3 Treating suppliers' intended price rises as a buying challenge and adopting one of several bargaining ploys:
   (a) threaten to change suppliers as a bluff,
   (b) change suppliers (but only temporarily),
   (c) delay the timing of price rises and insist on buying stocks before the price increase becomes effective.

Colorex adopts a buying strategy of trying to make its suppliers dependent on the customer by drawing them into a progressively dependent relationship, after which lower prices can be obtained. Suppliers are initially chosen for their capacity and delivery capability, provided that they are technically adequate; Colorex then insists on being treated as a "favoured customer" in any subsequent situation or shortage of supplies. Colorex appear to have a low regard for suppliers and considered many to be "almost as big crooks as we are."

This is then contrasted with another paint manufacturer, "Britapaints," whose supplier is a German company, Telford, Ltd.

Britapaints is completely dependent upon Telford for resin supplies, but this is deliberate. Telford undertake technical product and manufacturing development work for Britapaints and provide a very high level of technical advice, good service, and reliable deliveries. Britapaints trust Telford with a great deal of information of a commercial and technical nature about its own plans and developments in the industry; they have no reason to believe that this trust has ever been abused, even though the supplier also deals with other paint firms. The emphasis, here, is on source loyalty and the continuation of a long lasting, mutually beneficial relationship. . . .

> The German supplier undertakes a great deal of Britapaints' product development and they provide a great deal of reassurance to Britapaints in the suitability of their paints for special working conditions. Multiple sourcing by Britapaints is regularly considered but rejected on the grounds of high cost and poor use of its own resources. . . . However, it is not so much the products bought which distinguish the way in which the two paint companies interact with their suppliers, as their differing philosophies about their need to interact and their attitude to supplier relationships. . . . Britapaints operate in an "atmosphere of trust, co-operation, and vulner-ability" in the power relationship with suppliers, whereas Colorex generate an atmosphere of distrust and hard bargaining.

It appears to us that most of the very successful organizations in the West generally attempt to relate to their suppliers much more constructively—and not just because of the Pacific Basin challenge. Most have arrived at this relationship independently. They have done so because it is clear to their leaders that the relationships, internally and externally, need to reflect the reality of an economic *interdependence*. Consequently they have discarded the adversarial approach and have tried to install associative, joint problem-solving interactions with their key suppliers.

Insufficient credit has been given to the effective rela-tionship-building these corporations have succeeded with. It is no wonder that companies such as J. C. Bamford, Xerox, Ford, and ICL UK Ltd have become somewhat irate at the extolling of the Japanese as the exemplars of enlightened management. Having said that, however, there are far too few of these companies.

This chapter sets out to examine why there are so few, and to make a start at remedying the past. But first a recapitulation.

The final link in the strategy of competitive advantage is to build the right relationship with those suppliers whose services you value most. Those firms who are doing this are forging steadily ahead because it is part of a total rethink about the way they do business, i.e. the kind of relationship they need is integrated into an intelligent quality-improvement strategy, and it is not an instant solution out on a limb. But even more subtle than this thinking approach is a sort of inner orientation towards people, groups and relationships, which is to do with taking risks with people, letting go a lot more, trusting people and processes and *believing in ourselves* and not in robots, CAD/CAM, computers and the power of corporate PR campaigns.

The firms who are not taking this new approach are dropping steadily behind, and amongst these are many European firms. A case in point is the reluctance to adopt single supply sources where appropriate. *The Financial Times* of October 24, 1986 (Dullforce, 1986), published findings of Professor Ivor Morgan of Boston University (while he was at IMEDE, the international management training institute in Lausanne, Switzerland) wherein he insists that European manufacturers are throwing away a substantial competitive advantage by staying with multiple sourcing. Professor Morgan's frustration clearly shows through as he describes reactions of participants to his advanced manufacturing course as "severe indigestion." He cites logical reasons why the traditional relationship based on price and multiple suppliers is retained. Among other things it affords price control through competitive bidding, and reduces the risk of uncertain delivery because of labor disputes, accidents, etc. Underlying all this is simply the inability to form a relationship with another organization that is not punitive, contractual and, in a sense, inhuman. Professor Morgan speaks from experience, since his first job was with a company supplying pistons to British-based car manufacturers, and he asks the basic question—how to create the new relationship of trust and loyalty between supplier and manufacturer? But that particular question is premature because another question has to be answered first, and that is: what underlies our present mode of behaviour towards suppliers? Once we understand that then perhaps we can make a real start on the other.

We behave the way we do in business at least partly because we cannot bring ourselves to trust people enough. This is understandable and, infrequently, justified. Our defensive behavior, however, does not make for international competitiveness, particularly when it results in coercive contractual measures, which get in the way of developing productive relationships.

So the question has to be: how well-founded is the posture of our not trusting? Are people really generally untrustworthy, or is the beam in *our* eye, in that we are unable to bring ourselves to trust them? We think it is the latter and will now attempt to explain why.

WIN–LOSE IN BRITAIN AND THE USA

To demonstrate this there is an excellent exercise called Red–Blue, also called Prisoner's Dilemma, which we have presented to over 2000 negotiators all over the world. It is a game which demonstrates whether people display win–win (cooperative) or win–lose orientation (selfishly competitive) in a situation which offers the possibility of both. It contrasts their actual behavior with their expressed intentions, i.e. do people who say they support a win–win approach actually carry it out when the chips are down? If they do, the implication is that they will be equally concerned that the other party's needs are also met in any agreement.

The game has ten rounds and participants are divided into two groups to play each other. The objective is simple: "Your group is to get the highest positive score (by the end of the game)." This is done by choosing to play a Red or a Blue, the consequences of which are as follows:

Side A plays:

		Red	Blue
	Red	A Win +3 (red) B Win +3 (red)	A Win +6 (blue) B Lose −6 (red)
Side B plays:	Blue	A Lose −6 (red) B Win +6 (blue)	A Lose −3 (blue) B Lose −3 (blue)

The game proceeds through five stages.

1 Four moves played independently without a direct interaction with the other side, just transmission of each other's decisions.

2   A pause where there is the possibility of talking to the other side if *both* sides want this.
3   Four more independent moves.
4   Another pause with the possibility of interaction.
5   Two final moves whose scores count double, i.e. Red/Red is +6/+6, Red/Blue is −12/+12, Blue/Red is +12/−12, Blue/Blue is −6/−6.

Try it for yourself now.

THE RED–BLUE EXERCISE

Objective: End game with highest positive score for your team.
Rules:
1   There are two teams.
2   You will chose to play either **Red** or **Blue**.
3   You will be scored as follows:

Group A	Group B	Score A	Score B
Red	Red	+3	+3
Red	Blue	−6	+6
Blue	Red	+6	−6
Blue	Blue	−3	−3

4   There are ten rounds.
5   You can have a conference with your opposing group after the fourth round. (However, this can only take place at the request of *both* groups.)
6   You can have another conference after the eighth round, if *both* groups choose this.
7   The ninth and tenth rounds score *double*.
   • If both groups play **Blue**, each scores "**−6**"
   • If one group plays **Blue**, the other **Red**
      Red = −12; Blue = +12
   • If both play **Red**, each scores "**+6**"

Use the following scoresheet, and fill it in with an imaginary team on the other side in mind. After you make your choice try to complete their column objectively from this point of view. In particular think of the motives which govern your decision at round 8.

SCORESHEET

Move	Color played A	B	Score A	B
1				
2				
3				
4				

(Conference point)				
5				
6				
7				
8				

(Conference point)				
9 (double score)				
10 (double score)				

Totals

What did I learn: About my perceptions of the other party?

About myself?

How did you do?

The major learning point to emerge, which should be obvious from the beginning, is that there is no way you can end up positive without active cooperation from the other party. Given that information, anyone should be able to see that logically the procedure would be for each side to play Reds then they would both achieve their objective, i.e. ending with a positive score of +36 and +36. However, social reality in the business world is very different. People find it very hard to play Red and although there are differences across nations, especially between Britain and other Western countries, the same picture emerges. The outcomes among business people playing the game in our negotiation training programs in Britain and the USA are shown in Table 4.1.

Table 4.1 *Proportion of negotiators achieving the various outcomes*

Outcomes	Britain	USA
Win–win	12%	25%
Win–lose	75%	70%
Lose–lose	12%	5%

We can see that, far from recognizing the natural advantage of playing Red, teams tended to play Blue as many, if not more, times. Hence, the majority of the outcomes (75% plus) are either win–lose or lose–lose.

It can also be seen that the US participants were much more likely to achieve a win–win outcome than the British. This is even more significant in that the Americans in the research were given a briefing more likely to dispose them to a win–lose attitude than the British, who, despite being asked just to get a positive score for their team, are twice as likely as the Americans to get a negative score for *both* teams!

Why do we get these irrational outcomes? First of all, it is a cardinal principle in business life that "Uncertainty tends to produce conservative behavior." The main reason for playing a Blue is to *minimize risk*. The most you can lose is −3, and you have a chance of gaining +6. If, however, you play Red there is a likelihood of losing −6 with the alternative of only a moderate gain of +3 although it will be a mutual gain. And the sad thing is that even when people see that they are both going down the tubes with this negative spiral, they are still very often afraid to play Red. They just do not have the nerve to take a risk, become a little vulnerable, by trusting someone to demonstrate that there *is* another way. How often is this the case in real life?

In many ways the safest place to play a Red is move 1, after which there is plenty of time to recover by playing Tit for Tat. And here we find a really impressive difference between British and US participants.

The proportion of negotiators making an opening move Red (cooperative gesture) is

Britain	USA
15%	27%

This seems to indicate that a cooperative gesture is the least likely move for the British, while it is twice as likely for the American. The concept of winning, meaning the other person has to lose, seems to be more strongly grounded in the British and is perhaps related to their unwillingness to take a proactive risk. But even playing a Red at any time (offering cooperation and taking a risk) in the first four moves is something the Americans are far more likely to do than the British. In 60% of the cases the British did not play a single Red in the first four moves, while in 80% of the cases the Americans played one or more Reds.

The other interesting difference is the attitude towards the other side playing a Red. The Americans usually saw this as positive and were pleased by the development. The British, more often than not, perceived a Red from the other side with a sort of mild contempt, assuming that the other side had made a mistake and did not understand the game. A typical comment was: "Ah hah, now they've slipped up." With this attitude it is really not surprising so few Reds are played in Britain—unless, of course, you belong to the same old boy network and share the same club.

It is interesting to speculate where this attitude might come from. The first item of speculation must obviously be the class system. Some people would claim that the class system is alive and well, and that this explains the ambivalent attitude of the British to the concept of service. England in particular has a terrible reputation for service with the "obnoxious landlady," the "surly waiter" and the "snobbish shop assistant" epitomizing that peculiar capacity for making customers feel bad about themselves. The resentment and, at the least, the unease at serving people, make strange bedfellows with the customer service philosophy. And yet craftsmanship and engineering quality, which are in themselves a special kind of service, one step removed, still arouse great admiration in Britain.

So it seems that service is very often confused with servility. Why? Perhaps the answer lies in the attitude of those who receive the service, and is to do with the class system. Some of the worst experiences of salespeople and suppliers that have been recounted to us have been from those who have worked in Britain. Suppliers have been treated like serfs, and salespeople like intruders. In effect, in the Kantian sense, they have been treated as means to the buying firms' ends for far too long, and so in many cases a smouldering resentment has characterized the supplier's attitude, which has been reflected in the poor product quality and service produced.

However, perhaps the class system is not the only reason, if it is a reason at all. There is another conjecture: that the British do not really wish to take responsibility for a long-term relationship which is of relative equality. They actually prefer the arms length relationship, not because it is, on the face of it, more cost effective, but because they cannot risk "getting involved." There is a real anxiety about being my brother's keeper, feeling accountable for the well-being of another person, being open with them. It is safer to "play games," games with the unions, games with the organizational structure, games with suppliers and financial manipulation games, because then it remains merely an intellectual exercise and I remain comfortable.

This game-playing mentality seems to be at the heart of the win–lose behavior we saw so much of in Britain. Professor Wickham Skinner (1985) summed it all up very well, when, as a postscript to his review of the biographies of Iacocca and Geneen, he quoted Doriot's admonition "Make it or sell it' and then went on to explain that this suggested that:

> the heart of a business is the quality of its products and services, the real contribution it makes to customers and the society that must sustain it. Iacocca and Geneen and the events of the past decade demonstrate that Doriot was right and that if we are to recover the prestige and freedom of managers and public confidence in our business-centred system, we must earn it by going beyond the superficial professionalism of analysis and strategisms and financial manipulation to assuming genuine responsibility.

Happily our latest observations indicate that such win–lose behavior is decreasing in Britain, especially as different kinds of industrial leaders emerge such as Anita Roddick, Sir John Harvey-Jones, the recently retired Chairman of ICI, and Ben Thomson-McCausland of London Life. But it is still not fast enough.

THE CHANGES NEEDED

Given that people will only cooperate freely if they trust the other party, and given that, as so many people are saying, healthy buyer–supplier relations are crucial for competitive advantage, how on earth does the process begin? In a nutshell, it begins with leadership. The leaders of organizations must themselves change their attitudes towards suppliers; they must change not just their slogans, but their whole way of thinking about business. Then they can begin to create the kind of organizational conditions which discourage games playing, by themselves displaying, what Drucker (1982) calls "The Ethics of Prudence", where they have an ethical obligation to demonstrate correct behavior and avoid wrong behavior, including anything questionable. However, Drucker warns that the Ethics of Prudence, which go back to Aristotle, can easily degenerate into an hypocrisy of public relations, which employees are the first to see through. So the emphasis is not just on demonstrating the right behavior; but doing so continuously.

If there is incongruent behavior in an organization, then employees will employ their own minimum risk strategies and these will lead, as we have seen, into win–lose situations. The sobering thought is that when negotiators are challenged for behaving like this they defend it as appropriate, saying that they expected the other side to attack or not keep the agreement, so they felt they should get their retaliation in first! This means that people project their own anxieties, fears and negative values on to others; subconsciously anticipating behavior which they themselves are likely to exhibit. The number of times people acknowledge that trust is a key factor, and then go on to exhibit total lack of trust, because they simply do not understand what it means to exercise trust, is legion. The punitive contractual nature of so many of our agreements in the West are evidence of this, even though most buyers will admit that exercising their penalty clauses never really pays.

Just one final note to provide some comparisons which are not from Japan with our typical Western organization. In separate groups of women, and of blacks, in a large South African company, over 60% of the Red–Blue outcomes were win–win, and we have not yet experienced a lose–lose. This does not just say something significant about relatively disadvantaged groups and their greater awareness of the need for effective relationships to help them cope with inexplicable circumstances, it also reinforces our view of the way in which organizations can create an adversarial climate and shape the attitudes of people accordingly.

All this leads back to Professor Morgan and his urging for a reduced supplier base at least, and the trust and loyalty question. How does a corporation engender this kind of relationship? The answer is to have leaders who are not casuists,* who do genuinely believe in good supplier relationships, and to have strategies which help people change in order to implement these relationships successfully. We hope that this book will help to persuade and advise. But, before proceeding on this journey, you may be interested in reading this *Listener* review of Axelrod's book, *The Evolution of Cooperation*, which does convey the beginning of a strategy. It uses a slightly more elaborate version of the Red–Blue, called Prisoner's Dilemma, as its game, and contains some penetrating insights.

---

*Casuistry, used as Drucker (1982) used it, starting out as high morality, has become a rationale for leaders, in "conscience," to subordinate their interests, *including their individual morality*, to their social, or organizational responsibility.

Richard Dawkins: Co-operative evolution

The nice way to survive

Is being tough and nasty the way to survive, as neo-Darwinism suggests?
Dr Richard Dawkins reports on an alternative theory based on game-playing

'Nice guys finish last', part of the folk wisdom of baseball, was quoted by the American biologist and social prophet Garrett Hardin to epitomise the 'selfish gene' view of nature. The selfish gene view follows logically from the accepted assumptions of neo-Darwinism. It is easy to misunderstand but, once understood, it is hard to doubt its fundamental truth. Most of the organisms that have ever lived failed to become ancestors. We that exist are, without exception, descended from that minority within every earlier generation that were successful in becoming ancestors. Since all we animals inherit our genes from ancestors rather than from non-ancestors, we tend to possess the qualities that make for success in becoming an ancestor, rather than the qualities that make for failure. Successful qualities are such things as fleetness of foot, sharpness of eye, perfection of camouflage, and—there seems no getting away from it—ruthless selfishness. Nice guys don't become ancestors. Therefore, living organisms don't inherit the qualities of nice guys.

This logic is automatic and inevitable, and the Darwinian is bound, with however much regret, to dismiss 'the good of society' as a pie-in-the-sky irrelevancy in the ruthlessly individualistic world of nature. But the conclusion doesn't have to be so bleak as it at first appears. On the contrary, using a different definition of 'nice', one just as compatible with ordinary English usage, it is possible to derive from a fundamentally self-centred, Darwinian view of nature a genuinely optimistic conclusion, which sounds like the exact opposite of Hardin's. It is even possible to derive the motto 'Nice guys finish *first'*.

This alternative definition of a nice guy comes from the American social scientist Robert Axelrod, working in collaboration with the celebrated British evolutionist W.D. Hamilton. Axelrod's book *The Evolution of Cooperation* (Basic Books £13.50), published in 1984, may be one of the most important books on social theory ever written, although it has not been widely reviewed or publicised in this country.

A longtime favourite plaything of

game theorists is the so-called Prisoners' Dilemma. In the simplest version of this game, two players have each to choose between two moves. Cooperate and Defect (hereafter C and D). Unlike in chess or ping-pong, the players don't move alternately but simultaneously, in ignorance of the other's simultaneous move. If you and I both play C we get more (say £3) than if we both play D (say £2). If one of us plays C, and simultaneously the other plays D, the D player gets the highest possible score (say £4), and the C player gets the 'sucker's payoff' (say £1). So, from my point of view, the best outcome is that I play D and you play C. But if I calculate this, and play D accordingly, you are just as capable of working out the same thing and playing D yourself. In this case we both only get the low payoff of £2. If only we'd both played C, we'd both have got the comparatively high payoff of £3. But if I work this out and play C, you do even better if you choose D. We each calculate that, whichever of the two moves our opponent chooses, we are better off playing D. Therefore, rational players will always play D, and will always obtain the low payoff of £2. But—here is the paradox and the maddening dilemma—each rational player simultaneously knows that, if only he and his opponent could somehow manage to enter into a binding contract to play C, both would do better.

So far I've discussed the 'one-off' Prisoners' Dilemma, a simple version of the game in which no rational player will be a nice guy. The 'iterated' version of the game, however, in which the two players meet each other again and again, allows a richer range of strategies, based upon memories of past moves. For instance: 'Play C 90 per cent of the time, D on a random 10 per cent of occasions. If opponent plays D,

retailiate with two Ds in a row.' Notice that such strategies are precise algorithms that could be obeyed by an unconcious, pre-programmed machine, or by a brain whose behaviour was genetically pre-wired.

Can we discover which is the 'best' strategy? This is where Axelrod came in. He ran a competition, inviting computer experts from around the world to submit strategies for winning the Iterated Prisoners' Dilemma game. In the main round of his competition, he received 63 strategic programs. He fed them into one big computer and let them loose against each other, over hundreds of repeated rounds, in all 3,969 pair combinations, to see which would win. But the 'winner' is not necessarily the one that amasses the most points in a naive football league-table sense. Alexrod and Hamilton defined 'success' in a more sophisticated Darwinian way. Strategies in Axelrod's computer didn't win money, they won reproductive success. The computer game ran for a number of 'generations', and in each generation the number of copies of each strategy reflected its success in previous generations. Successful strategies came to dominate the population; unsuccessful strategies eventually went extinct. It follows that, to be permanently successful, a strategy has to have what it takes to do well against copies of itself: successful strategies dominate the population, and therefore provide the most probable opponents of any given strategy.

Remarkably, the winning strategy turned out to be the simplest of all the 63 submitted. It was called TIT FOR TAT (henceforth TFT). TFT begins by playing C. Thereafter, it always simply imitates the previous move of its opponent. In other words, it plays C unless provoked by a D, in which case it retaliates once.

Axelrod defined a 'nice' strategy as one which is never the first to defect. TFT is a nice strategy. It is also 'forgiving'. A forgiving strategy has a short memory for the opponent's past misdeeds. Having retaliated once, firmly and unambiguously, TFT then wipes the slate clean and lets bygones be bygones. Other strategies are nice but unforgiving. For instance, I invented a strategy called GRUDGER, which remembers all individuals that have ever played D against it, and plays D against them forever. Some other strategies are not nice: they sometimes play a gratuitous, unprovoked D, thereby winning a high score in the short term, but probably reaping vengeance thereafter. What Axelrod found—it is only with hindsight that I am not surprised—was that nice, forgiving strategies in general, and TFT in particular, consistently did better than nasty ones.

Why, then, do nice strategies do so well? Because they help each other to amass large scores. To use another of Axelrod's engaging technical terms, TFT is not 'envious'. Unlike almost all humans that have ever played the game, it doesn't try to beat the other player. The other player is treated not as an opponent, but as an accomplice. It is remarkable, though obvious when you think about it, that neither TFT, nor any other nice strategy, can ever actually win a game against an opponent. It often loses, and it can never score better than a draw, because it is never the first to defect. The reason nice strategies can still end with more winnings is that their drawn games are high-scoring games, their lost games are low-scoring. While nasty guys win low-scoring games, nice guys quietly get on with accumulating their winnings in unspoken collaboration.

This agreeable conclusion only follows if the conditions are right. The game has to be 'non-zero sum', which is another way of saying that winning for one player is not synonymous with losing for the other. The payoffs have to be those defining the Prisoners' Dilemma. The 'shadow of the future' has to be long. This means that the players have to meet over and over again— 'iteration'—and they must do something equivalent to recognising each other as individuals. Fortunately, a wide variety of situations, both in human life (for instance in First World War trenches and the modern arms race) and in biology (for instance, in the relationship between figs and wasps) are fundamentally equivalent to a (very likely unconscious) Iterated Prisoners' Dilemma.

Without ever appealing to unworkable ideals of species welfare, universal altruism, or the 'rights' of all, a simple computer game has shown how fundamentally self-interested entities can work towards amicable collaboration, and has shown that the qualities that make for individual success in at least some areas of a fundamentally competitive world are niceness, a lack of envy, and forgiveness. TFT takes an optimistic view of its opponent, is always ready to initiate a new round of co-operation, and, after one swift and firm retaliation, is ready to forgive and forget. And it is these very qualities that earn it its individual success.

Now, will somebody please translated Axelrod's book into Arabic, Hebrew and Russian, and prepare a comic-strip summary for the White House?

Richard Dawkins, author of 'The Selfish Gene', presented 'Nice Guys Finish First' for 'Horizon' on BBC2. His new book 'The Blind Watchmaker' is published by Longman.

(reproduced by permission of The Listener*)*

SELECTED REFERENCES

Dawkins, R. "The Nice Way to Survive," *The Listener*, April 17 (1986).
Drucker, P. F. *The Changing World of the Executive*. Heinemann, London (1982).
Dullforce, W. "A Singular Way to Increase Competitiveness," *Financial Times*, October 24 (1986).
Hakansson, H. (ed.) *International Marketing and Purchasing of Industrial Goods by the IMP Group*. John Wiley, Chichester (1982).
Skinner, W. "Make it or Sell it—Don't Keep Track of it," *Harvard Business Review*, September–October, pp. 36–40 (1985).

5
The Development of Organizations—and the Implications for Buyer–Seller Relations

Now what is this growth? Is it a reality or not? Yes, it is a kind of reality. It is the reality of the quantitative aspect of the world. . . . The other part of reality is development. . . . This requires a quite new concept of management, of co-operating, of leadership.

(*Lievegoed, 1979*)

Whenever we look at organizations we tend to see them as static entities—as illustrated by most pyramidal organization charts—straight lines depicting and enclosing functional positions. (Have you ever seen a chart with curved lines?) Unfortunately this does not capture reality, life *is* untidy, boundaries are always being moved and, like everything else that lives, organizations tend to change, constantly. The question therefore is, is there another way of looking at our organization which can help us make decisions for its future? One answer is to look at it from a *developmental* perspective. This means understanding the laws of development and using these to diagnose the present and then to deduce a probable future with the intention of influencing it.

Here is a quick run down of these laws.

1 Development is discontinuous.
2 Development occurs over time in a series of stages.
3 Within each stage a system appears which has a structure characteristic of that stage.
4 Crisis periods appear between each stage, when one dominant quality is redundant and the next one has not yet emerged.
5 Development is not reversible.

What does an organization look like, using this approach, and what are the implications for our business relationships? We will examine these, leaning very heavily on the work carried out by Dr Bernard Lievegoed and our associates at the NPI Association in Holland. But before we do, we would first like you to complete the following questionnaire, and then check your answers at the end of the chapter once you have read it.

DIAGNOSTIC EXERCISE FOR YOUR ORGANIZATION

Please read the following seven statements, each of which has three possible answers. Decide which answer you think suits your *ideal* views best. Try to describe why, and/or under which conditions or circumstances. Then try to find the answer that most closely represents the *real situation* in your organization, and give the reason why. (This may be difficult as there can sometimes be overlap, but try nonetheless.)

The objective of this exercise is to become aware of the differences between your ideal views of your organization and reality.

After you have completed the questionnaire read the chapter through and then score your answers on the score sheet at the end of the chapter. You may want to compare your observations with those of colleagues to obtain a more rounded feel for your organization.

1 Efficiency is brought about by:

1   Attracting those people whom one can trust to know their business and their job and to give of their best talents out of loyalty towards the firm.
2   Setting up systems which carefully monitor and control all aspects of the business. Standardizing procedures and ways of working. Saving on human labor as much as possible.
3   Developing human and capital resources on a continuous basis. Establishing relationships with the client field which enable us to respond effectively to their (situational) needs.

Our ideal choice is for _____, because:

Our present practice is most like option _____, because:

2 Selecting and promoting staff

1   My key managers have had special training in interviewing techniques, so that they can practice our main policy, which tries to explore with the candidate to what extent job and person fit together. A joint conclusion, giving reasons, at the end of the interview is preferable to a little "thank you" note three weeks later. We apply the same priciple in relation to promotions. We find that this approach makes us attractive to good candidates, and gives employees confidence.
2   That is an issue in which I want to be personally involved. When I have a good interview of 30 to 45 minutes I usually have no difficulty in making up my mind. I make a special point of their background and whether they have had the right kind of practical experience. I do not believe in psychological tests and all that stuff.
3   This is primarily an issue for the specialist. My managers see to it that applicants for non-managerial jobs have the proper qualifications. For managers I need a more thorough investigation: records and references are carefully checked and as character is so important I take great heed of the advice of a psychologist.

Our ideal choice is for _____, because:

Our present practice is most like option _____, because:

3 Public relations are best handled when:

1   I have an open-door policy towards customers, suppliers and the community. I rely on the good reputation the firm has built up over years by giving personal care and attention to my clients' needs. This provides a solid basis for our firm and will always earn us the respect of the community.

2   Our own sense of identity is the key to our relationship with others. We have to agree—as partners—what should be the nature of our professional services in relation to the field of clients. Both our specialized professional skills and our style of working are important in this respect. In an open and exploratory style we and our constituents should jointly and regularly review whether we still have the right level of response to their needs. "Bad news for us is then as important as good news." They are both challenges for our development.

3   I carefully keep track of all (business) developments within the community. I make use of all data local and national institutions can give me about changes in the marketplace and use modern marketing techniques. We make a special effort to have high visibility with potentially big customers. Advertising, if done professionally, will give us new opportunities.

Our ideal choice is for _____, because:

Our present practice is most like option _____, because:

4   In our opinion leadership in the organization means:

1   To give the right instructions and orders to the right people, to tell them in broad outlines how it must be done and how one likes it to be done. Then allow the people involved a large amount of freedom to execute the given instructions in the way one would like things to be done oneself. For this, strong leadership on essential points is necessary, because people have to know what they are up against. It is also important to know one's subordinates very well.

2   To see to it that everybody receives the right instructions and that these are forwarded through the formal channels. The clearer and more detailed the instructions are, the better the job will be done. It is also essential that all subordinates are treated according to the same standards, to avoid envy and favoritism.

3   Showing subordinates as soon and as clearly as possible what are the aims and policies. They will then be able to judge for themselves what relation exists between their own job and the job of others. Furthermore, it is important to see to it that subordinates are trained sufficiently to perform their tasks satisfactorily. Regular work discussions with subordinates is a means to get to know them well and helps to raise the team spirit.

Our ideal choice is for _____, because:

Our present practice is most like option _____, because:

5   In our opinion top management must consist of:

1   A team of able managers, who, on the basis of their different expertises, decide their division of labor amongst themselves. In setting goals and aims for the firm, as well as in deciding company policy, decisions have to be made unanimously. Leadership within the team will be mainly functional leadership, which means that all team members are individually responsible for the decisions made by the team. Within their own task areas the different team members are free to make individual decisions as long as they adhere to agreed policies.

2   A group of different specialists. Specialism means clear division of tasks. Well-defined job descriptions are absolutely necessary. One member of the group has to be (formally) the leader of the group, because one must be able to turn the scales when the votes are equal. If not, decision-making becomes very difficult, which can damage the interests of the firm.

3   One strong person who is responsible. They must know everything that is going on in the company, more or less in detail, because otherwise they are not able to make the right decisions. This kind of management is the most successful.

Our ideal choice is for _____, because:

Our present practice is most like option _____, because:

---

6   In our opinion the best way to delegate is:

1   To make a clear plan of how the work should be executed. Then the instruction, based on the plan, is given to staff. Give them some space to work out the plan and finally supervise the result and correct where needed.
2   To give instructions to staff as follows—tell them roughly what we want them to do, giving them freedom in how to implement this. Afterwards only check whether the way it was carried out is meeting our standards of the job.
3   To tell staff clearly what the goals of the job are. What the demands are, the conditions and our policy. Within this scope they are free to handle the job as they like. Only check to see that it comes up to agreed standards. As manager one is not in the first place responsible for how subordinates handle their jobs in detail, but for delegating jobs only to those that can handle their responsibility and are trained well enough to do a good job.

Our ideal choice is for _____, because:

Our present practice is most like option _____, because:

7   **If one has to solve a problem it is our opinion that the best way is:**

1   To think it over by oneself. See what experiences one has of similar problems and then make a decision. Tell your subordinates what decision you have made, so that they will be able to act accordingly. If you are not able to solve the problem by yourself, the best way is to say to your subordinates: "This is the problem, see that you solve it!" Afterwards you have to check of course whether this has been done.

2   Check for yourself which people or what specialists one has to consult. Then talk the problem over with each of them separately. As soon as the different aspects have become clear to you take all of them into consideration and weigh them. The decision that you take will then be communicated to your subordinates. You also make notes about this solution so that in similar cases you can take the same decision.

3   To get your subordinates together for a staff meeting and tell them what the problem is. Together you try to analyze the problem, its causes and the consequences of alternative solutions. The insight you get will enable you to find the right criteria for the solution. As soon as you have agreed these criteria, you choose the best solution in this situation.

Our ideal choice is for _____, because:

Our present practice is most like option _____, because:

PHASES OF ORGANIZATIONAL DEVELOPMENT

Looking at Figure 5.1 you will see that the organization moves, as it grows, through three phases; pioneer, rational/scientific and integrated. Each phase has its own characteristics, reaches a peak before declining and then has to come to terms with its inadequacies (crisis) before growing stronger. This process of development has implications for every aspect of the com-

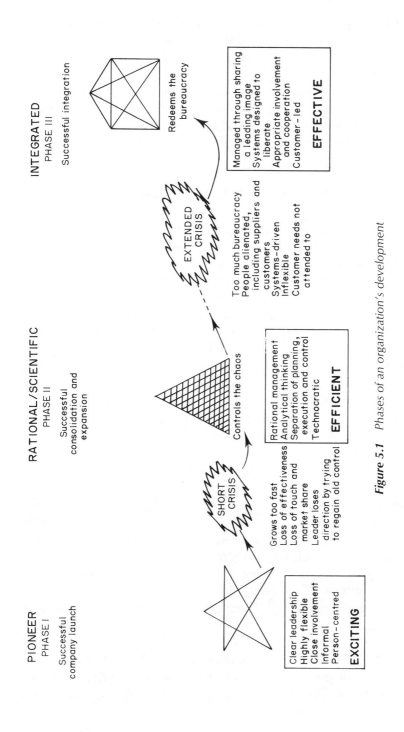

Figure 5.1 *Phases of an organization's development*

pany's operation, not least of all its style of management. This creates a ripple effect, and the one ripple we will look at now is the impact on your supplier.

It is a fairly safe hypothesis that there is a direct correlation between the way an organization behaves internally and its behavior towards its suppliers. So, using the developmental model as a basis, let us examine the organizational context of buyer–supplier relationships.

THE FIRST PHASE: PIONEER PHASE

The starting point of many organizations is the "one-man-show" and entrepreneur. We define an entrepreneur as someone who is frustrated by the imperfection of the world. They envisage an improvement and are convinced that their capacities will create a product, a service and money.

The pioneer has not yet a clear goal, but rather an idea. The motivating force of the pioneering phase of development is these ideas. The pioneer usually starts out by tapping personal resources and relations. They have friends and relations and warm them up for their ideas. Their first markets are old relationships, friends, etc., and this is carried into the organization. Their first suppliers often became friends or close associates. It is recorded that Henry Ford's battery supplier was puzzled by the curious and very precise specifications for the wooden cases in which four batteries at a time were to be shipped. Then one day he pulled back the rubber floormat on his new Model T and recognized one side of his shipping case as the floorboard of the vehicle. Mr Ford's concept was to have only one or two first-rate suppliers for each key commodity who would be closely integrated into the design and manufacturing processes in order to avoid waste of resources or talent at the intermediate steps. His close collaboration with Harvey Firestone contributed directly to the advancement of tire technology.

The strength of the pioneering entrepreneur is that they know all the people in the company and much of their important public outside the company. They do not need specialists; these would constitute blind spots in the organization, because they cannot be motivated by the pioneer's personal willpower. For the same reason the pioneer does not manage according to hierarchy. Managers and supervisors are frequently bypassed because the pioneer tends to talk to everyone and anyone. The marketing approach is by frequent personal contacts with customers, because inside the company the pioneer is a craftsman, outside a merchant.

A healthy pioneering organization is strong because of the following characteristics:

- Leadership is clear, the leader's judgment is trusted.
- There are clear goals and attention is paid to consumer needs.
- People are committed.
- Products are either innovative or high quality.
- The pioneer trusts his own judgment in choosing his allies.

Dominant Relationship

The pioneer creates a production and service-driven culture, e.g. small computer firms and specialized component suppliers. The dominant relationship is that of *trading*, and the behavior that of open persuasion within and without the organization, characterized by enthusiasm, energy and product knowledge at all levels. As production and buying are not yet clearly differentiated, purchasing tends to be less formal and divided quite specifically into

(a) high volume, cost-centered "as needed" transactions and
(b) high value, technically customized interactions conducted by the pioneer directly with senior levels of selected suppliers.

At its best the relationship is a typical needs-based trading situation which works beautifully with smaller suppliers and buying organizations; but which can create all sorts of problems with the larger, less flexible, bureaucratic type of organization. The pioneering supplier is very often appalled at the complexity and rigidity of the buying procedures that confront the company; just as the larger buyers are frustrated by the demanding and seemingly irrational behavior of the pioneer.

The same sort of dilemma often occurs with the larger suppliers, whose salespeople are product-orientated and whose supply systems are much too rigid for the pioneer type of customer. So, very often the pioneer will encourage a number of smaller subcontractors to set up around the main organization to supply the more customized products in a flexible way. This is what Sir Clive Sinclair did in Cambridge as he built up his then successful computer organization, Sinclair Research. This is a hitech example of what Naisbitt (1984a) would call networking, and it represents the interdependent relationship at its best.

At the other end of the scale the pioneer organization is quite prepared to haggle seriously about the price/cost of standard goods or services. This can come as a shock to the somewhat unidimensional corporate person who expects a degree of homogeneity in business behavior. So problems will tend to occur between the Pioneer and Rational organizations, and not with the Integrated organization which is more flexible—and very rare.

The Crisis of the Pioneer Phase

All institutions in society started more or less as pioneering organizations. One often observes pioneering *styles* in the sales or research functions of companies. They often preserve an intuitive, improvising and person-orientated style of work. Sometimes one observes the pioneering style not only at top management level of a large enterprise, but also at the bottom, for example in the repair and maintenance department, particularly in the interpersonal relations between bosses and subordinates. The same applies when a new subsidiary comes into being, or when a new specialism is initiated, for example, a training department. In all of these cases, the skilled eye sees many characteristics of the pioneering style. The question may be put: when is it that this style is no longer adequate and must be replaced by the next higher form of organization? The answer is:

(a) When the number of employees, the scope of production and the increasing size of the market are violating the managerial principles of the pioneering phase; i.e. with growth.

Adaptec sprang its leak early in 1984. In one quarter, Adaptec's three biggest customers, all fledgling micro-computer-related companies, stumbled and abruptly canceled their orders. Wiped away in one stroke was 50% of Adaptec's revenues. Almost immediately, inventories surged to $6.7 million—compare that figure with the $6.3 million that represented Adaptec's entire sales for the fiscal year ended Mar. 31, 1984. The company's cash balance shrank to $131,000.

The smell of disaster focused Boucher's mind. He had, he discovered, been so obsessed with growth that he neglected to put controls in place to manage the results. There were no regular meetings among Adaptec's marketing, sales and manufacturing staffs to refine production forecasts. Finances were so disorganized that the company was not verifying shipments coming in against purchase orders. Suppliers were shipping parts Adaptec didn't need and back-ordering parts it did, and the company didn't know any better. Receivables were bumping 100 days. Admits Boucher: "I didn't know what I was doing."

(*Forbes* magazine, 1987a)

(b) When the succeeding generations take over. Pioneers are often capable of managing larger organizations than their successors because they were there right at the outset and because their mark is left on everything that has developed. For the successors the company is less comprehensible. They cannot manage from within but have to do it from above. Looking at the company from the top downwards or from the outside the company is a "jungle" of people, odd tasks and work-methods, etc., and this creates an anxiety which the original pioneer did not have, and is often compounded by inadequate management who have not developed under the pioneer.

Symptoms of an "overripe pioneering company" are: mishandling of finances, loss of quality, delivery mistakes and high insecurity. Usually one "smells" the crisis all around the place.

The message for the buyer? If the relationship between the pioneer and buying company is sound and the quality good, go in and help. This is usually best done by backing off with procedures and instead providing counsel and objective advice. The worst thing to do is back them into a corner with threats and pressure, because for a healthy development the next phase should be entered, and they may just need your help to make the transition.

THE SECOND PHASE: RATIONAL/SCIENTIFIC PHASE

The Rational Rationale

The principles of rational or scientific management as attributed to Frederic W. Taylor at the beginning of this century are *mechanization, standardization, specialization* and *coordination*. The principles of that dreaded word "efficiency."

The principle of *mechanization* was not new, but it gained momentum when the principle of *standardization* was applied. Batch-order production of equal parts became possible and the productivity of machine output was accelerated. A classic example is that of Henry Ford introducing mechanized and standardized quantity production, and Haskell and Barksdale of Du Pont mechanizing in order to reduce the number of accidents.

The principle of standardization and normalization yielded excellent efficiencies and was also applied to the workers. They became involved in a process which has been called the mechanization of the organization. Interchangeable standard parts and standard quality norms, standardized achievement norms, standardized classification and appraisal procedures, standard instructions, appear on the scene out of such institutes as Du Pont's Labor Efficiency Unit which, in 1912, set out four principles of "Scientific Management in Powder Making."

By applying this principle of standardization throughout, the complicated pattern of activity within a company becomes predictable and can be rigidly controlled. By initiating norms, future action is fixed. This explains why *planning*—which in fact is essentially the controlling of time—is becoming all important in the second phase. Often planning becomes predominant and the real objective of the organization is obscured. The real objective, after all, is to satisfy the needs of customers. Compare this state of affairs with the pioneer who was, so to speak, in daily touch with customers!

The danger of the second phase is that the real needs of the customer—fixed in products produced by a mechanistic organization—tend to be forgotten because meeting the norms of planning has become the all-important goal. The supplier is trapped in the same net as procedures take over from human contact with buyers. Now the next two points are exemplified in J. Alfred Sloan's classic organization plan of 1920 which succeeded in bringing order to a fast-sinking General Motors in the wake of the chaos left by the pioneer Durant.

Specialization is the third important characteristic of this phase. People and functions are forced to focus their activity on a limited field. This results in quality improvements backed up by scientific methods and an increase in production output, due to "going through the motions of a well-planned scheme." No longer are suppliers chosen on the judgment of the pioneer, but more likely on the results of a more formal bidding process which tends to leave the final choice up to the market, usually as a result of emphasizing cost in competitive bidding.

Coordination arose because the leaders of scientifically managed organizations understood quite well that the introduction of the artificial boundaries of specialization violated the "natural cohesion" in existence during the pioneering stage. They envisaged that the centrifugal forces of differentiation could seriously damage the efficiency of a rationally constructed organization. Consequently they introduced this fourth centripetal principle of coordination; the most important characteristics of which are:

- *Staff-line division*: a major problem arises with the increasing number of specialists who know more and more about less and less. This tends to fractionate the organization. The "solution" is found by introducing the "staff-line" notion. Specialists are attached to staff departments giving "advice" to the line. The classic example was Sloan's division of operational general managers supported by a highly skilled general advisory staff corps. The advisory staff were consultants, and prerogative of command was dictated by the line managers.

- *The span of control*: each manager should have a limited number of subordinates in order to control and coordinate their work personally.
- *Controlled wages by incentives*: introduction of achievement norms and relating achievement and remuneration makes it possible to mobilize human energy for the enterprise by appealing to "own interests." It boils down to the "money and motivation philosophy." The Du Pont bonus plans were some of the earliest examples of this policy in action—to discipline the men to obey especially the safety rules. This same approach is used towards suppliers in the belief that money is sufficient motivation to assure the desired performance, thus inappropriately addressing "existence needs" when, in fact, the supplier is looking for satisfaction of "relatedness" needs and even beyond.
- *Communication methods*: a complicated network of information distribution is needed to inform management about the work activities of employees in order to insure that they meet the prescribed standards of planning and achievement and to inform the employees about plans made by management. Consequently formal communications multiply.
- *Instruction and training*: labor needs to be formally trained to carry out the work prescribed by the organization in a systematic, controlled way; but often getting "fixed" in this type of mechanistic method when others are more appropriate.

Given this greater control, the second phase type of organization is in a position to manage a much larger "field" than that of the first phase: a larger and more diversified production program, a larger market, in short a more complex enactment of *rationalization*.

Rationalization usually leads to centralization and an institutionalized hierarchy of people, who, within a relatively short space of time, can point to the "visible" effects of their efficiencies, i.e. reduced costs, increased margins and controlled growth. New catchphrases spring into being such as "competitive drive," "market share" and "economies of scale." These are the first signs of a psychological withdrawal from concern for consumer needs being uppermost, as they (the consumers) must also be controlled—as must the suppliers—otherwise they could interfere with the efficient running of the organization. Nevertheless they are right. Profits often soar when the second phase gets into gear; and that is what the organization needs.

Relationships inside the company are clearly defined and departments keep each other strictly at arms length. The complementary side of all this is that there is a great deal of visible, written communication and instruction, so that you *see* the information generated and also, thereby, control other departments and protect your rear at the same time. Information is jealously guarded and becomes a highly negotiable item because it reflects the power structure.

Dominant Relationship

So, with relationships and information thus structured, the major interactions in this kind of organization are likely to be cold-blooded *negotiations* and lobbying—very often in a distorted form—because, although on the surface pragmatism is the name of the game, what actually is rewarded most often is outsmarting and manipulating the others. And successfully negotiated outcomes are very often not that at all; they are much more likely to be dependent on the power ratios and sponsors. They tend therefore to be win–lose, with long-term lose–lose implications. Both Lee Iacocca and John De Lorean identified this in Ford and GM. And at that time, their two organizations were not renowned for their fairness to suppliers.

How does all this affect the purchasing department? In two ways:

1 They do not get all the information they need, especially as regards lead times for new developments, when they are

very frequently told too late to elicit maximum contribution from key suppliers. In fact, David Burt and William Soukup (1985) have concluded that "the most vulnerable aspect of the product development system in many companies is their failure to use the full creative capabilities of potential suppliers."

2   Suppliers too are caught in this web of competitiveness and manipulation, where power is covertly the real independent variable; a situation exacerbated by the frequently perceived lowly status of buyers. This is reflected by them to their suppliers, often disguised under the pseudonym of price.

Interestingly enough, being powerful as a consequence of representing a powerful organization seems to rob buyers of a degree of consciousness, so that quite often they do rather inhuman things to suppliers like Jerry (inset story). When confronted by their power in action (otherwise called force), they are genuinely surprised, or even hurt. And they seldom realize the degree of resentment created in the supplier by this behavior, which is perceived as a callous dismissal of the supplier's needs.

What makes some of the suppliers really angry, however, is the number of publicly uttered pious slogans by the very large rational organizations, such as "we care about quality, in our products and in our relationships," "we encourage our suppliers to treat us as partners in a joint venture," etc. At the receiving end the supplier often feels humiliated by the attitude of the buyer, and manipulated by the cold pragmatism of the firm, which very often means that in good times the supplier is pressured by delivery demands and in bad times by price—no matter what their so-called partner may be saying publicly (utterances which often make their own buyers cringe as well!).

So it is no surprise, therefore, that vendors are mistrustful, thin-skinned, and often downright hostile, especially with the up-market, merchandise buyer, who, peculiarly enough, seems to have a status outside the company (high) that is inversely related to their status in the company, until they reach a middle management level.

A young merchandising buyer in a very large retailer, who had been dealing with an entrepreneur, Jerry, who ran a very profitable small business, and who displayed his success, justifiably, with his Porsche, beautifully tailored suits and second house on the coast, was amazed when, at the beginning of the annual round of negotiations, Jerry announced that he was quitting. When the buyer relocated his bottom jaw and asked why, Jerry replied: "Look, I am a successful person. I pay one and a half million pounds in salaries every year. Over two hundred people depend on my decisions and energy for their livelihood, and a lot more in the small city where I live depend on them. My working week is seldom less than seventy hours, not counting travel, which is made a lot more pleasurable because of my Porsche. My community respects me, and I feel good there. *But*, when I come here, and to other such buying organizations, I am not shown respect, given consideration or time. I am just given business, and that quite condescendingly. Now, after eight years, I have had it. I am selling out and someone else can handle the hassle. And I just thought you should know personally; so I came to tell you—goodbye."

In fact, the buyer is as much a victim of these circumstances as the vendor, but not as conscious of it. When we have probed buyers in the rational/scientific organizations we have uncovered insecurities, feelings of powerlessness, and occasionally feelings of guilt, which contrast strongly with the perceived super-confident postures when they are negotiating. They are often the meat in the organizational sandwich, and there is often no way that they can allow themselves to listen to the real needs of their suppliers until the organization is so arranged that this becomes legitimate. And this brings us to an examination of the crisis of this phase.

The Crisis of the Second Phase

The second phase, as it has been described, is a necessary condition for any company to operate in a larger and more complex world. The managerial principles of the second phase may operate quite satisfactorily for some time. The principles when applied promote the expansion of the enterprise.

Often the so-called "informal organization" (encompassing many relics from the pioneering stage) helps to eliminate the "razor's edge" of the second-phase set-up. Gradually, however, a number of phenomena appear on the scene indicating that the scientific management approach cannot be perpetuated eternally. The following problems can be observed:

- *Freezing*: the assumptions of the second phase are that markets, products and people are rather static. Standardization and specialization therefore often result in bureaucracy and a "freezing" of the organization, so that one of the dangers of the second phase is that the organization becomes *static*. This may hold true for their marketing approach, product development and personnel management, which do not adapt to outside developments. Relationships with suppliers will most likely be shaped by the *positions* of both parties, rather than by their true *interests*.
- *Leadership and coordination*: the centrifugal forces of specialization may lead to subspecializations on a scale so big that coordination becomes impossible. Departments and functions drift apart and do not understand each other's roles. Communication is ever more difficult because each specialist area has its own language. The overall objectives are obscured and departmental empire building tendencies are reinforced by the setting of their own targets. Coordinating committees, liaison officers, and what have you, emerge. They usually cannot solve the real problems. At this stage the cry for "strong management" is often heard and this may lead to a regression into the pioneering phase.

Usually outsiders step in as the executive talent inside is promoted into top positions in their domain, often after a long and specialized career. They are then, as is explained, not qualified—because of age and experience—for the "generalist top positions."

This second phase is often autocratic by nature. The higher commands and controls the lower. This results in blocked communication channels upwards and downwards; higher up, for example, one knows less and less about what really happens down the line. Coordination is more difficult. Down the line it is difficult to see the broad picture and people find it hard to "delegate upwards." At the top the responsibility for problem-solving and decision-making accumulates. Down the line there is mental apathy and very few initiatives are taken.

Along with this development, the overhead costs increase and control of these costs is progressively more difficult.

- *Motivation*: one of the most serious, pathological symptoms of the second phase is the diminishing commitment to work achievement. The illness starts out at the bottom on the shop floor, spreads to the offices, to the research laboratories and affects the salesforce and may even penetrate the highest levels of management. People start to leave, especially the best. The causes are many: people feel their work to be relatively useless, and become alienated and divorced from meaningful high quality effort. *And this includes suppliers,* who feel that what they have tried to do has not been recognized and their needs not acknowledged.

- *Staff-line*: the staff-line construction, built on advice and command, proves to be an unworkable construction. The expertise of a staff member is often such that their advice is perceived as a command. In their own domain the experts have line authority. In reality the line managers are frequently used by their colleagues in an advisory capacity. In practice it becomes increasingly obvious that the distinction between staff and line is artificial. As long as this distinction remains untouched on paper, the problems between staff and line will continue.

Buyers very often have a particular kind of problem in this last regard when headcount or other considerations dictate that procurement for line manufacturing operations should be conducted from a division or corporate staff department. They may have a significant impact on the margins of the line activity, but are viewed as likely to be uninterested in helping the line managers meet their immediate needs. This can lead to poor communication, bickering over performance, finger-pointing and general lack of trust as line managers tend to feel that only the people who report to them can be expected to pursue their operating objectives as vigorously as they themselves do. This can make it particularly difficult to coordinate the purchase of commodities common to more than one operation in multiplant firms.

Here are some typical comments from the buyers:

"If you want to get along, learn how to work the system." This means that the customer and supplier come last as you start doing the right things and not doing the things right.

"There's too much empire-building going on, and it is mainly in staff areas."

"It takes ages to get management to act on intelligence from the field, mainly because it takes ages to get it to them in the first place. So we are losing contact with the customer, and others who can react faster to their needs are taking the business."

All this occurs because of two major flaws.

1   Far too much attention is paid to the organization itself—it becomes introverted.
2   Interference is created in the lines of communication by too many specialists, committees and reorganizations, which makes the organization clumsy and inflexible in responding to the outside world. Chrysler in the 1970s was a typical example, as were British Leyland and British Steel, and US Steel. Here is an example from USX, again taken from *Forbes* magazine (1987b).

> For the last decade Roderick has fought to dismantle USX's legacy, what Morgan and Gary called "a rounded proposition," a fully integrated steel giant with seemingly inexhaustible supplies of iron ore, limestone and coal, which were mined and transported to the mills by the company's huge shipping fleet and its own rail lines. "Circumstances have changed," Roderick says. "How much iron ore does Taiwan own? How much coal do the minimills own?" So Roderick has trimmed USX's wide-ranging operations, selling $4.7 billion in assets, from coal reserves to timberland, while writing off $3 billion more. Within two years, he says, he hopes to sell another $1.5 billion.
>
> Analysts estimate that as recently as 1982 USX was losing $125 for every ton of steel it produced.

And as a result of these the organization loses sight of its purpose—to serve the customer and satisfy the stockholder—something which they often do not notice until too late. Those readers in supplier organizations who work at this interface and who, therefore, impact on customers (and vice versa) may well have experienced those feelings of great frustration, which the above obstacles to good buyer–seller relationships can generate. If so, we sympathize. However, while it is true that the organizational structures of the bureaucratically organized firm work largely against any development of the associative relationship, the good news is that it is possible to make very substantial progress, given the right kind of leadership, as we have demonstrated in Chapter 4, if the rational/scientific organization will loosen up, so that it can develop towards the integrated phase without too much turbulence. And this means redeeming relationships at all levels by first making people conscious of how they are working. This should be done through a systematic careful process, led by the top executives, and not by a wild Utopian leap into participation— usually preceded by an edict from the top: "You WILL be participative; end of discussion!"

Let us finish the study of the impact of organizational development on the buyer–seller relationship by examining the third and least-frequently found phase—that of the integrated organization.

THE THIRD PHASE: INTEGRATED PHASE

We can summarize the deterioration of the second phase development into two concepts: *freezing and isolation*. The company at this stage is unable to cope with the dynamics of change. To overcome the problems of stagnation and isolation top management needs to think of *regenerating productivity through people again and through organizing the processes more effectively*. This, effectively, is Total Quality.

It is not necessary for both these approaches to start from scratch. After all, in the second phase, a fair amount of human-relations and public-relations work will have started. Task analysis, job descriptions and functional blueprints have arrived on the scene. Process analysis, routing schemes and work flow-charts are in operation. All these things are in fact typical products of the second phase organization. Processes and relationships are analyzed, quantified and schematized according to a rational model. People are fitted in. In the third phase, the essential thing is *the way in which* relationships and processes are engineered, and *the way in which* people are fitted in. The approach taken determines whether these processes and relationships are handled as "open systems"—open for innovation and development—or as "closed systems." It is in fact all about *quality*, or what David Hurst (1984), in a most thoughtful *Harvard Business Review* article, defines as what happens "between events." He uses a practical table to differentiate the two phases. He describes his original company as operating with a conceptual framework which was a "hard" rational model, typical of an organization dominated by the rational approach. He puts this hard "box" at one end of a spectrum, the other end of which is, what he describes as, a soft "bubble" context, and does so because, when trying to manage efficiently, one must know which framework is dominant at that time.

Now it is important to realize when studying the framework in Table 5.1, that Hurst is an experienced executive, not a theoretician, who has collated the terms out of his painful

Table 5.1

[box—p2] **Tasks**	[bubble—p3] **Roles**	[box—p2] **Information processes**	[Bubble—p3] **Networking**
Static	Fluid	Hard	Soft
Clarity	Ambiguity	Written	Oral
Content	Process	Know [seeing]	Feel [ing]
Fact	Perception	Control	Influence
Science	Art	Decision	Implementation

[box—p2] **Structure**	(bubble —p3] **Groups**	[box—p2] **People**	[bubble —p3] **People**	[box—p2] **Strategy**	[bubble —p3] **Mission**
Cool	Warm	Rational	Social	Objectives	Values
Formal	Informal	Produce	Create	Policies	Norms
Closed	Open	Think	Imagine	Forecast	Vision
Obedience	Trust	Tell	Inspire	Clockworks	Frameworks
Independent	Autonomy	Work	Play	Right	Useful

experience of trying to manage in a merger which could have been a disaster.

The "boxes" in the left-hand columns describe the features of a second phase, rational/scientific organization very well (p2), while the right-hand "bubbles" describe the next phase of development (p3).

In this next phase relationships and systems are supported by people who understand the complexities of interdependence, and also take the risk of basing their cooperation on the expectation that the other party will respond to a win–win gesture. By developing this trust they create space for effective functioning. A condition required to make this work is a profound insight into the nature of interdependent relations and the characteristics of interfunctional and interpersonal trust and candor. One of the first insights in this respect is the notion that trust and confidence cannot be organized or constructed, but must grow out of a continuous process of development of interpersonal relations. This applies inside the organization to work groups, departments, hierarchical levels, etc., and is equally valid for relations outside concerning suppliers and stockholders. For key suppliers this constitutes something of a return to the relationship they enjoyed with the pioneer, in which their special efforts to help that pioneer were clearly reciprocated.

The Process Organization

Between the various participating groups in your organization many interactions occur. Flow of goods, rotating people, information streams, cashflows, money circulation, etc., are just a few. In fact it is quite possible to look at an enterprise as an extremely complicated mixture of processes (as is done in operations research) varying from cyclical to one-off processes, from short- to long-term processes. For example, time-spans could range from the one-day process for handling correspondence in the typing pool, to management development processes taking as long as ten years. It is customary nowadays to understand a company and each of its constituent functions and departments as an "input–output" system.

We prefer to refer to them as "customer–supplier" systems:

a notion that is finding increased favor with those organizations working out of Total Quality. From this point of view it is irrelevant whether the organization unit is a foundry, an accountancy or a training department.

In this third phase it is of the utmost importance that management and employees find a new approach to many of the second phase techniques, methods and procedures. [This was what Hurst (1984) found his merging organization had to do.] In cybernetics we work with the principle of "closed circuits." In our approach to organizational development we employ the idea of open systems or "bubbles." The importance of an open system is clear when one recognizes that any organizational process is a subprocess of something larger, and consequently must be subservient to it. For example, the handling of correspondence in the typing pool of the purchasing department is a subprocess of the total function of purchasing. Purchasing, yet again, is subservient to production. Production is only a subpart of a large process beginning with the needs of the customers and ending with their satisfaction—marketing. Each process must be receptive to input from above and to change from within. Technology changes, people change—the whole process must remain dynamic to be effective!

The key characteristic of this kind of organization is its end-user orientation, which is genuinely needs-based. The consumers are not a variable to be manipulated by clever marketing ploys. They are regarded as human beings who have wants and aspirations, and are given the same attention that (it is now realized) people in the organization demand. Product emphasis is on quality, not on volume, price or clever features, and this is a result of a level of awareness of *service*— that ultimately as an economic institution you are there to serve at all levels, from stockholder to customer. If you respect people, this service is quality-driven. A good example of where this is now happening is in IBM.

In fact, we have much to thank the whole computer industry for; because the very esoteric nature of the product and its extraordinary power (thanks to the microchip) has meant that consumers have had to be wooed—products are judged by their consumer 'friendliness,' and ethics, in the broadest sense, has come back forcibly into business consciousness. Silicon

Valley has not just produced the most amazing technological insights, but also, as a result, some really clear, illuminating social insights, which indicate a high level of social and relational consciousness. We have found that some of the most challenging writing about the meaning of being a human being at work has come from those who have been through the crucible of the computer and software production world.

Now, despite all that has been written about companies that are 'excellent' in the now-popular use of that word, these integrated organizations are few and far between. In fact, some of the best examples are not the business headline-grabbers. They tend to have a lower profile, which is not related to their extraordinary growth or profit-sharing, but rather to their steady progress and enlightened relationships both inside and outside the company. If anything, these firms are recognized by their ability to puzzle people and to make analysts wary as they are hard to classify along the traditional taxonomies.

Perhaps the best general example is one generated by Drucker (1980), when he postulates the "transnational" model for the future. He says the cohesion will come, not from the control of capital; but from control of marketing, or customer orientation. New structures will be required where, instead of the pyramid organizatic n, with top management driving a large number of units through centralized control, it will, instead, act as an integrating force. ("It will need an orchestra rather than an army.") John Naisbitt (1984b), in *The Year Ahead—1985*, makes much the same point when he observes that managers are becoming trainers and mentors, not controllers.

Enlightened negotiations, which help move a second phase organization towards the third, integrated, phase, lead inevitably to a climate of trust in the organization. This radiates out to the environment and starts the process of association between the supplier, the manufacturer/retailer and the consumer. So the active relationship between supplier and purchaser becomes one of "association," characterized by the ability to conduct joint problem-solving exercises on a whole variety of issues, but all ultimately designed to maximize consumer satisfaction.

Naisbitt states how important the consumer has now become

and quotes a 1977 Lou Harris study "Consumerism at the Crossroads." This concluded that companies have a decade, or less, to begin including consumers in the corporate decision-making process—or face aggressive new consumer action. Naisbitt goes on to say (p. 178) that he cannot understand why producers are not engaging their consumers earlier in the production process. He then postulates that perhaps corporations are simply scared because they do not understand participatory democracy. We think he is right, but that he has only touched on half the issue. The other half is at the supply end, with companies consulting *their suppliers* openly and early. Not until this is done is the chain complete.

So, what is the problem? It is two-fold:

1 Our top management are not always sufficiently conscious of what it really *means* to be responsible for a big business. There seem to be two reasons for this:

   (a) They do not understand sufficiently how organizations and people really work. Whether or not they are aware of it they usually operate out of very simplistic, almost mechanical, models. This can be very confusing for their managers because, at one level, the executives talk as if they do know what makes the organization tick, while at the same time, at another level, they fiddle and tamper with the structure and alter direction in such a way as to effectively demonstrate their real ignorance of what causes things to work well in their own company.

   The confusion thus caused is compounded by inevitable meaningless but arresting slogans which accompany the changes. It is almost as if the executives are working out of some unsubstantiated theories about how organizations work. Rudolf Steiner (1980) wrote: "If a man feels a lack in a particular field he begins to spin theories about it." This does make a lot of sense in today's business world because everything is changing so quickly and radically that people at the top are confused and are unable to cope. Hence they construct their own reality or theory which produces a situation which, false thought it may be, is one they can understand.

Unfortunately, their judgments arise out of old habits and thinking; and while they may be convincing themselves that they are leading the organization into the future in the right way, all they are in effect doing is making themselves intellectually more comfortable. The organization becomes their construct of reality and a great deal of energy is put into making sure this is accepted (woe betide those who point to the fact that the King really does not have any clothes!). Ultimately their theories destroy reality, and everyone in the company starts to wander about in a fog of resigned rationalization, knowing in their hearts that it is not going to work and that they are about to undergo one reorganization after another. You can almost see creativity, energy for the task, and motivation stream out of them.

This phenomenon is evident in parts of the British Civil Service today, as the theories of the various political incumbents about society, organizations and people very often take what the civil servant has to administer further and further away from the real needs of that particular sector of society.

There is also a tendency to set new policies which demand that Civil Service departments emulate private business. Unfortunately, the models used are obsolete, emphasizing as they do internal competition and cost-cutting (efficiency!). These are not the attributes of modern quality-driven organizations. This is sometimes accompanied by a de-valuing of whatever was done in the past as being inefficient, and indeed even uneconomic (!) at times. This is a technique which is distasteful, as it is merely an act of vanity at the expense of many hard-working people's sense of self-worth. If the majority of the British senior civil servants were not generally such genuinely dedicated people, who manage extraordinarily well under most difficult conditions, some of the political masters would be cruelly exposed for their egocentricity. And the same goes for some private organizations. The people at the top of these do not seem to recognize the extent to which their theories (particularly about reorganization) are propped up by those below them.

(b) The second reason for this lack of consciousness at the top is that the inevitable survival mechanism of rationalization in a manager becomes casuistry in an executive.

Indeed, Drucker was sufficiently concerned about this to dedicate an entire chapter in *The Changing World of the Executive* to discussing business ethics (1982). What he is discussing, in fact, is moral responsibility, and this only arises from an increased level of consciousness that business leaders need to work on before they can operate associatively—the preferred mode of phase three (see Figure 5.2)

2   Having an "associative" relationship means that the purchasing company will be giving away power, as this is part of developing trust. These are very emotive issues because, in effect, this means relinquishing that feeling of direct control, which is so dear to the company bureaucrats and pioneers. It means, as a purchaser, that you can no longer do as British Leyland and Ford did in the 1960s and 1970s, when the competition really got tough, and threaten suppliers if they do not perform at *your* required level. Because the relationship is two-way they will come straight back with what they expect of you, and what their expectations are of your minimum levels of performance, and where you have fallen short. If you are unable to handle being treated as truly an equal, then all your slogans and public relations aphorisms will avail you nothing; and, as we have seen from the Red–Blue outcomes, the British in particular, seem to shy away from taking responsibility for that kind of egalitarian relationship.

Joint problem-solving activities are obtained between partners in a venture, *not* from a perceived authoritarian relationship where the supplier is just another resource. It is just as true for two business firms as it is for two individuals, that "morality is the business of treating other people as ends in themselves, rather than as objects or means," to quote Kant again. If you have led suppliers to expect peer treatment and you cannot deliver, then you are back to well below square one in terms of trust and cooperation. It is a long haul to re-establish that level of trust.

IMPLICATIONS FOR BUYER–SUPPLIER RELATIONS

Having now established what phase you think your organization may be in and what the implications are, it is time to examine the consequences for the vendor relationship.

The likelihood is that you are in a phase two, rational, organization, where the emphasis is on keeping costs down, tolerances tight and deliveries smartly on time. Most supplier relationships will be strictly contracted, and new work will be initiated by tender, with cost being the main criterion—even though slogans such as "quality counts" and "leading edge of technology" may be popular. And in this systems-led, cost-conscious environment both supplier and buyer may be trapped in a strictly functional relationship.

Very often under these circumstances it is the suppliers who, because they are at the receiving end, are the most obviously frustrated. The buyers do, however, let their frustrations show occasionally, especially when they discover that certain tolerances demanded are too strict, or certain specifications too high, for the life of the product. And they become especially frustrated when they know that a particular supplier is just right for their company, because that supplier really understands the company's needs, but cannot exploit this ability because of management's demand for three bids, or because of some other cost criteria. In this they actually become quite a lot like some of the development engineers who *know* which supplier is technologically best for their product development, but are not allowed by the system to put that supplier's name on the drawings.

When the frustration starts to run high it is, peculiarly enough, again the supplier who suffers the most. The purchasing department finds it too painful to handle the contradiction between policy and best practice so what it often does is to minimize risk and fall back on price-driven policies. These give them the excuse to quote rules which obviate any real human relationship with suppliers. This reduces the buyers' stress caused by the inner contradiction because they can point at the policy and say: "Sorry, these are the rules and as much as I would like to I can't make exceptions." This is a relational crisis

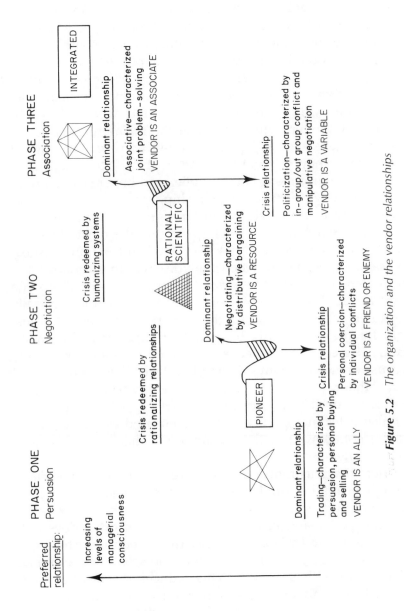

Figure 5.2 *The organization and the vendor relationships*

point, and if you refer back to the diagram (Figure 5.2), phase two crisis, you will see what it can do to the supplier.

It is here that the phase two organization is becoming unhealthy, and these behavior symptoms of an even more instrumental buying–selling relationship—where people are treated as things—constitute one of the first signs. Sometimes this distorted relationship is also a result of an economic squeeze, and it is one of the most sure-fire ways of ensuring that you will not get preferential treatment from your suppliers at the time you need it most.

What the organization needs to do is recognize the reality that these bureaucratic activities are actually beginning to get in the way of effective business relationships (especially close relationships, as are demanded by just-in-time manufacturing)—and to stop forcing a false reality on the situation, which leads to so many win–lose exchanges, just because of this need to be procedurally comfortable in the midst of so much contradiction. This is where negotiation really comes into its own as a device for raising the consciousness of all concerned, especially of the internal functions on whom supplier performance will impact. The issues are no longer the preoccupation of the negotiation. The focus now becomes the relationships, and the question that should be uppermost in everyone's mind is: "What kind of relationship do I need with my suppliers to best get done what needs to be best done?"

It will have been seen how negotiation works as a transition phase in changing the relationship in a healthy way and why it is vital to understand this if your organization is going to get the cooperation it needs. Basically there are two routes an organization can follow, as Figure 5.3 illustrates.

If the buying strategy is to concentrate on "subduing" its suppliers, then what the buyer will get will be a compliant supplier who, at the very least, is unconscious of the buying organization's real needs and, at the worst, is hostile to them. The negotiations will be conducted either in a coldly contractual manner, with each side minimizing risk in relationships and substantive issues, or in an overly hostile way with the two negotiating sides looking for opportunities to score off each other (to play a Blue). Either of these two outcomes leads to a

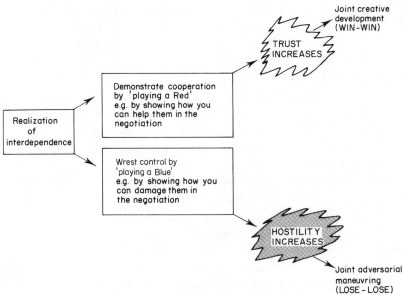

Figure 5.3

deformed interaction which contains no risk-taking and thus allows no growth or development for anybody.

If, however, the buying strategy is cooperative then there will be innovation and quality, expansion and development, and, ultimately, very satisfied customers. But a cooperative buying strategy is not enough for successful implementation. For this an organizational strategy is needed. So the next chapter will discuss a vehicle which can be developed to take you more safely past all those organizational dragons that seem to be blocking the way to the associative relationship.

ANSWERS TO DIAGNOSTIC EXERCISE

Method

Please transfer your choices to the columns below. The columns *are reversed* so put your answer to the "ideal" question in the second column, and your answer the "present practice" in the first column. Just circle your choices.

The third column is for you to put in your own reasons why you have chosen to move from one phase to another. We have inserted common examples to guide you in doing this.

Meaning

1   If you have identified the same phase in five of your seven present practices then there is a very strong likelihood that that *is* the phase you are in. If it is four or less then you are probably in a transitionary phase and lack a clear common culture.

2   If you skip a phase then you are apt to be a little Utopian in your desire for quick change, as the laws of development rule that an organization must pass through successive phases just as a child must when moving from pre-pubescence into adulthood.

3   If your ideal means moving back a phase then you are being nostalgic, because again the laws of development rule that regression is not possible. It is, however, a great opportunity to examine why you feel the way you do, i.e. has the organization tried to skip a phase and caused disorientation?

4   If your options stay the same, i.e. ideal and present practice do not differ, your organization is stable and effective where it is.

	Present practice	Ideal	Explanation for ideal option
1 *Efficiency*	*Option 1* Pioneer	*Option 2* Rational/ scientific	Example: We need to be less reactive and have more clear systems so that we can plan and use our time better. Your reason:
	Option 2 Rational/ scientific	*Option 3* Integrated	Example: There are too many procedures which slow things down and hinder individual initiative. We need to loosen up. Your reason:
	Option 1 Pioneer	*Option 3* Integrated	See **Meaning** 2 (*above*)
	Option 2 Rational/ scientific	*Option 1* Pioneer	See **Meaning** 3

	Present practice	Ideal	Explanation for ideal option
	Option 3 Integrated	*Option 2* Rational/ scientific	See **Meaning** 3 (*page 91*)
	Options stay the same		See **Meaning** 4
2 *Selection and promotion*	*Option 2* Pioneer	*Option 3* Rational/ scientific	Example: Personal relationships figure far too high in the selection and promotion process, and there are too many square pegs in round holes. We need some clear job definitions. Your reason:
	Option 3 Rational/ scientific	*Option 1* Integrated	Example: The whole recruitment and promotion process is far too cumbersome and slow, and often it takes months to be able to offer someone a job or to get an early promotion. We need some flexibility and new ideas. Your reason:
	Option 2 Pioneer	*Option 1* Integrated	See **Meaning** 2
	Option 3 Rational/ scientific *Option 1* Integrated	*Option 2* Pioneer *Option 3* Rational/ scientific	See **Meaning** 3
	Options stay the same		See **Meaning** 4

	Present practice	Ideal	Explanation for ideal option
3 *Public relations*	*Option 1* Pioneer	*Option 3* Rational/ scientific	Example: We are too busy to listen to our "public" and we do not store the information properly. We need to put someone in charge. Your reason:
	Option 3 Rational/ scientific	*Option 2* Integrated	Example: We have too much research data and no one seems to be doing much with it. Very often it just states the obvious anyway. We need to reexamine the needs out there—personally. Your reason:
	Option 1 Pioneer	*Option 2* Integrated	See **Meaning** 2
	Option 3 Rational/ scientific	*Option 1* Pioneer	See **Meaning** 3
	Option 2 Integrated	*Option 3* Rational/ scientific	
	Options stay the same		See **Meaning** 4
4 *Leadership*	*Option 1* Pioneer	*Option 2* Rational/ scientific	Example: Leadership is too unpredictable because it seems to be dictated by whatever are top persons' key interests. We don't really know where we are going and what the most important policies are. The need is for a corporate plan. Your reason:

	Present practice	Ideal	Explanation for ideal option
	Option 2 Rational/ scientific	*Option 3* Integrated	Example: We are led by systems, procedures and reorganizations. The executive is far too remote so they don't realize how much company politics goes on. We need some vision and excitement. Your reason:
	Option 1 Pioneer	*Option 3* Integrated	See **Meaning** 2 (*page 91*)
	Option 2 Rational/ scientific *Option 3* Integrated	*Option 1* Pioneer *Option 2* Rational/ scientific	See **Meaning** 3
	Options stay the same		See **Meaning** 4
5 *Top management*	*Option 3* Pioneer	*Option 2* Rational/ scientific	Example: The managers are spreading themselves far too thinly and are all trying to do too much. They will not tell us clearly enough what they want. There also seems to be quite a lot of open disagreemet and argument at the top. We need to be less anxious and have some planning frameworks for consistent management. Your reason:

	Present practice	Ideal	Explanation for ideal option
	Option 2 Rational/ scientific	*Option 1* Integrated	Example: The managers are bureaucrats. We have endless meetings with far too many presentations requiring all sorts of data-gathering—and then a decision is not made for a long time anyway. We need more imagination. Your reason:
	Option 3 Pioneer	*Option 2* Integrated	See **Meaning** 2
	Option 2 Rational/ scientific	*Option 3* Pioneer	See **Meaning** 3
	Option 1 Integrated	*Option 2* Rational/ scientific	
	Options stay the same		See **Meaning** 4
6 *Delegation*	*Option 2* Pioneer	*Option 1* Rational/ scientific	Example: Delegation is not precise enough, and it often seems based on what the boss does not like to do. So people often set things wrong, are severely criticized, and have to put in a lot of extra work to put it right. We need some clear objectives and standards. Your reason:

	Present practice	Ideal	Explanation for ideal option
	Option 1 Rational/ scientific	*Option 2* Integrated	Example: People are not given any real authority. They do not seem to be trusted to do more-important things. We need some new ways of doing things. Your reason:
	Option 2 Pioneer	*Option 2* Integrated	See **Meaning** 2 (*page 91*)
	Option 1 Rational/ scientific	*Option 2* Pioneer	⎱ See **Meaning** 3
	Option 2 Integrated	*Option 1* Rational/ scientific	⎰
	Options stay the same		See **Meaning** 4
7 *Problem solving*	*Option 1* Pioneer	*Option 2* Rational/ scientific	Example: Too many problems are not being attended to, and those that are are not being really thought out. So we are doing things which we know at times are pretty dumb. What is needed is more consultation on the *real* problems of customers and suppliers. Your reason:

Present practice	Ideal	Explanation for ideal option
Option 2 Rational/ scientific	*Option 3* Integrated	Example: All the problem-solving is in the hands of the specialists and people feel alienated. There is quite a lot of bickering and infighting. What is needed is some cross-functional group work. Your reason:
Option 1 Pioneer	*Option 3* Integrated	See **Meaning** 2
Option 2 Rational/ scientific	*Option 1* Pioneer	
Option 3 Integrated	*Option 2* Rational/ scientific	See **Meaning** 3
Options stay the same		See **Meaning** 4

SELECTED REFERENCES

Drucker, P. *Managing in Turbulent Times*. Heinemann, London (1980).

Drucker, P. *The Changing World of the Executive*. Heinemann, London (1982).

Lievegoed, B. *The Developing Organization*. Celestial Arts, Millbrae, CA (1980).

Lievegoed, B. *Towards the 21st Century: Doing the Good*. Steiner Book Centre Inc, Vancouver (1979).

Forbes, July 13, p. 40 (1987a).

Forbes, July 13, pp. 75–76 (1987b).

Hurst, D. "Of boxes and bubbles, and . . . effective management." *Harvard Business Review*, Vol. 62, No. 3, pp. 78–88 (1984).

Naisbitt, J. *Megatrends*. Futura, London (1984a).

Naisbitt, J. *The Year Ahead—1985*. The Naisbitt Group, Washington (1984b).

Steiner, R. *Threefolding–A Social Alternative*. Rudolf Steiner Press, London (1980). (From lectures given in 1922.)

6
An Organizational Strategy for Developing Buyer–Supplier Relationships

There can't be a Silicon Valley without a Detroit.

(Lee Iacocca)

The concept of phases of organizational development put the finishing touches to the situation in which an organization finds itself. The other factors of competition, suppliers and personal psychology have already been covered. We are now ready to look to a strategy for developing relationships across the buyer–supplier interface which completes the chain linking primary producer to satisfied customer.

The key issues are risk and trust, and the organization itself is responsible for creating the conditions within which they arise. So the first step in any strategy of cooperation here is to evolve one around the organization.

THE FIFTH CONSTITUENCY

Rosabeth Moss Kanter (1985) reports in *The Change Masters* that the Business Round Table issued a new statement on corporate responsibility in 1981, which declared: "more than ever, managers of corporations are expected to serve the public interest as well as private profit. Four "constituencies" were identified—customers, employees, communities and society at large, and shareholders . . . (some progressive companies add a fifth constituency: suppliers)."

The notion of "preferred supplier" is becoming common parlance today and it is the fifth constituency in action. In some companies, such as IBM, Xerox, Ford and Honeywell, it is an operational policy. In others it is a twinkle in some key executive's eye and thus it is at those uncertain crossroads where it can become either a living statement or a meaningless slogan. Avoiding the latter means breathing life into it by, as a start, taking into account all the steps we have so far indicated:

1   Recognizing the consistent need to enhance or, at the minimum, maintain the other party's self-esteem.
2   Using negotiation as a tool to develop the relationship, not as an autonomous activity.
3   Being aware of the forces that work against developing relationships and encouraging trust and risk to overcome these.
4   Accepting that organizations, as they grow, pass through qualitative changes, called "phases of development," which have implications for the kinds of relationships that will most likely arise between suppliers and customers.

Not to recognize and work with these, and other changing relationships, is to merely pay lip service to the notion of improving external relationships. The first people to suffer from this will be the buyers and the suppliers, because there would be a lot of mixed messages from the various interfaces, causing mistrust to grow at every meeting. The result would be, instead of improved relationships, a *deterioration* as increasingly suspicious suppliers and increasingly confused buyers retreat into their minimum risk postures. In short, the whole process of entering into this "new form of partnership" (as Bob Galvin, Chairman of Motorola, calls it) demands a lot more imagination than merely going out with a well-scripted policy statement.

THE CHALLENGE

Developing this "imagination" is no easy task, because it means going far beyond just structural changes. It means understanding the new *forms* required, not just the new structure: forms of relationships, of communications and of interactions that people accustomed to dealing with suppliers merely as means to their firm's ends will initially find very difficult. It often helps to have a strategy to work from when charting unfamiliar territory and here is one which has proven very successful both at the formal and informal levels in an organization.

First of all, let us be clear what we understand by "strategy." We can do this by comparing it with "tactics:"

Tactics

In military terms, tactics refers to "maneuvering forces in the presence of the enemy, or within range of his fire." Tactics, in relationship-building, refers to specific decisions taken with the other party in support of a given strategy, i.e. behaviors.

Strategy

In military terms, strategy refers to "the operations or movements previous to a battle." In relationship-building, strategy refers to positioning of each party for sustained influence on the other.

Basically three substrategies used to be considered in any effective change process. They are associated with the hierarchy of the organization, and with the roles and responsibilities attached thereto, i.e.:

- *Mega-strategy*: positioning in the industry sector and in society.
- *Macro-strategy*: positioning within and between organizations.
- *Micro-strategy*: positioning at the interfaces of working groups.

The mega-strategy

This is the statement of the concepts and ideas for the future (the vision) which form the new policy, such as, for example, "establishing a network of preferred suppliers who will want to give us a level of service which considerably exceeds the standard for the industry."

However, these ideas are usually not thought out beyond the slogan stage and then what happens is that the embryonic mega-strategy is translated via directive into a micro-strategy, i.e. the buyers must now conduct "better" negotiations, improve their interactions. A lot of energy goes into telling the buyers and suppliers about the new vision, and into public relations. Despite all of this, it is seldom seen to get off the ground. This is because it has not been thought through *deeply* enough, particularly at the relationship level. In a rational organization, most human processes tend to be treated much like production processes—almost in spite of everyone's best intentions. Usually the "how to do it" is left entirely to the buyers, or at least to the buying organization, who are often being asked to make great changes in their orientation without being given the right help so to do.

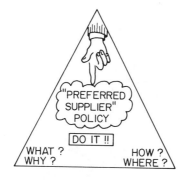

Figure 6.1

THE SOLUTION

The answer is to derive a macro-strategy which is concerned not only with the new idea, but also with the effective implementation, or translation, of it into useful action. And the best vehicle for the enactment of this is a group which will act as the organ for breathing life into the ideas and for giving direction and impetus to the actions. For the time being let us call this a "mediating group." To understand how it will work calls for a different approach to the way in which we see organizations. Instead of looking at an organization as a structure fixed by reporting lines, hierarchy and functions, let us use a more organic model and examine it as a process, fluid and moving, as was shown in Chapter 5.

Instead of the ideas or plans going straight from top to bottom through all those layers or segments in Figure 6.1, which so often filter out the meaning, the mediating group acts as the "heart" of the process. It takes in the plans, greatly improving their feasibility by resolving functional differences on criteria, minimum acceptable goals, interpretations of standards, etc. It feeds back improvement and/or agreement, and then circulates them to the "limbs" in a way which enriches their meaning and purpose. In this way, words and wishes are transformed into purposeful and enlightened action.

This mediating group thus becomes central to any effective change process because not only does it bring a precious judgmental

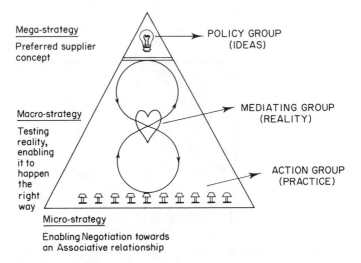

Figure 6.2

quality to that process, it also shortcuts all those strata so common in rational/scientific organizations which so often distort, or filter out, the original meaning. The change then happens in the way it was intended.

Many writers are currently concerned about the one-sidedness of merely "head" or pragmatic thinking, and the bias that this seems to induce into decision-making. Some, like Peter Drucker, deplore the immorality of the decisions this seems to produce, while others see it more as a block to the manager's own personal growth, as it produces a one-sided person, concerned only with cold analysis. We have experienced both these conditions and have come to endorse a balance of head with *heart* thinking because head thinking alone does not seem to produce the most effective decisions in the relationship area and in most areas of business policy. This was recognized in the editorial of the *Harvard Business Review* (1985, number 1) which stated that "a little knowledge of the sophisticated technique counts less than intuitive judgement, informed, but not enslaved, by analysis."

When organization executives want change they too often expect individuals to just get on with it and alter their behaviors accordingly; the reasoning being that the *knowledge* that they should change should be sufficient to produce different behaviors and attitudes. This deception prevails in spite of repeated examples of the opposite, i.e. people clinging stubbornly to old ideas and habits, despite some considerable suffering at a personal level, and others just playing at the changes. Our experience suggests that the mediating group will remedy this by acting as intermediary between the thinking (the executive) and the acting elements (the buyers and others down the line), so that proposals would be based on realistic judgment, and the ensuing actions would have the right quality. This then becomes a learning loop mediated from the center, which leads to even the most revolutionary idea being permeated with reality, and the most mundane new activities being directed out of a sense of the whole.

We will now look at where to set up this forum and how it will work to develop the potential of the buying and selling relationship. But before we do this, let us reexamine some of the realities.

In the end, the customers must pay all costs and provide all margins accumulated in the manufacturing process from Mother Earth to themselves. It may be temporarily possible to push a given added cost back on a supplier, but ultimately that supplier must be compensated for all expenses, plus a return satisfactory to the owners, or they will at some point cease to function. On the other hand, it is generally true that the market will allow the producers in this manufacturing chain to retain any cost reductions beyond those needed to keep the product competitive at the consumer level. This provides a powerful incentive for those producers to work collectively, wherever possible, to reduce those accumulating costs as the components (and ultimately the end product) move through the various steps from extraction to completion. This should be the most frequently found *common ground* between industrial buyers and sellers—the desire to reduce the cost of "their" product (or to improve their collective chances of landing the consumer sale which pays them both). But, persuading the parties to work together at each buyer–seller interface up and down the manufacturing line for the good of all, is far more difficult to achieve than to describe.

It turns out that suppliers, just like any individual, will look after their own needs first and foremost, whatever they may be. This seems to be true in all cultures, and is neither good nor bad, simply a fact which can be used in efforts to influence them, or ignored at your own peril. Let us repeat the simple, but profound conclusion, that *"your ability to influence another party is very largely determined by their* perception *of your willingness to help them meet their needs."* Note that it is their *perception*, and not your real intention, that is governing here. If this gives you pause, bear in mind that the exact reverse is also true. The other party's ability to influence you is very largely determined by whether or not you perceive their *actions* as working in your interests as well. The road to hell is paved with good intentions, partly because intentions are not visible—actions are—and unless there is a clear link between what you say and what you do, people will remain unconvinced.

Because suppliers are (a collection of) individuals, striving to meet organizational "selfish" needs, it follows that they can best be influenced by those customers they perceive as willing to help them meet those needs. Notice that we are discussing needs, not wants. It is extremely rare that both parties in any buy–sell transaction will get every little thing they may have wanted. But it is essential, if the transaction is part of an ongoing relationship with a key supplier or customer firm, that each perceives that their minimum needs are being met in an ongoing way at every significant point of contact with the other party's organization. This means not just with buyers, but with engineers, cost estimators, quality assurance representatives and so on. Suppliers respond to their own "consequences system," meaning that they are conscious of the results of their actions. They endeavor to repeat those actions which they can see bring desirable results, and they tend to avoid those actions which bring undesirable results, as measured against their own needs. To repeat, this is neither good nor bad, but if you want sustained change from them, it is a fact which can be made to work for you. When ignored, it will more often work against you.

Accepting this, a fascinating question for the customer firm, which wants its key suppliers to do things for it that they do not do for everyone, becomes "how to be, and *to be perceived* by these 'preferred' suppliers as, genuinely offering a win–win relationship?" The answer comes in four parts:

1   By ensuring that their own senior management truly want to help suppliers meet their needs. The best way of doing this is by orchestrating a meeting between suppliers and key executives.
2   By maintaining an internally consistent communication and decision process, which constantly reinforces that desire to see the key suppliers' needs met, so long as those suppliers feel equally keen about seeing the customer's needs met.
3   By ensuring that the people in all interfacing disciplines have the skills to determine and deal with the underlying needs (not positions) of those key suppliers.
4   By maintaining an ongoing audit process which measures relative success or failure in the above—especially as seen by those key suppliers—in order to generate a continuously improving relationship (more on this later).

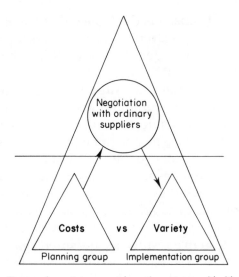

Figure 6.3   *Design for minimum risk and maximum likelihood of conflict*

For a given buying or selling organization in the manufacturing field, the group dominating the negotiation planning may well be composed largely of financial types, whereas the implementation group is nearly always dominated by line manufacturing and distribution (see Figure 6.3).

Too often, this results in a failure to consider all of the needs of the implementing groups in the resolution of the issues. The buyers are often acutely aware of this conflict, and feel disabled as a consequence. They then often adopt a minimum-risk style, because they know that when implementation group needs are not fully met, individuals in the implementation group will tend to resist carrying out the agreement—and they are the very ones on whom *everyone* must rely for faithful execution of the details of any agreement reached. Furthermore, their failure to implement will likely be perceived by the other party as a failure of the person who negotiated the agreement (the buyer and the seller), and that person's credibility (trustworthiness), and therefore effectiveness, will be damaged accordingly. All of this is especially bad news for a buying organization which is endeavoring to influence its preferred suppliers to do things for it which they do not do for their other customers.

The solution to this dilemma, insofar as *preferred* suppliers are concerned, is found in bringing the planning and imple-

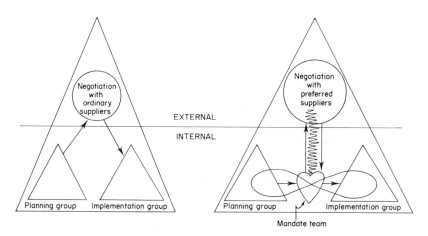

Figure 6.4 *Bringing the planning and implementation groups together*

mentation groups together—at least through representatives if not actually—before any effort is made to resolve a given issue involving them. The model of such an arrangement would look something like Figure 6.4.

This melding of the will of the planning parties with the needs of the implementing parties into a cohesive "mandate team," as we call it, has an immediate payoff; it becomes the ideal support group for the negotiator. The results should be exceptionally clear goals for the negotiator to pursue, and a much more confident negotiating stance. It should be easy to determine when the conditions require a negotiating *team* rather than an individual negotiator because of complexities, scope, etc. (When a team is indicated, it should ideally be drawn from the mandate team itself.) The increase in the confidence level of the negotiator is enormous when all needs are well represented in the room during the actual negotiation. To risk agreeing to something which does not satisfy some point in the mandate is substantially reduced. Best of all, the likelihood of encountering difficulty in later selling any marginal points of the agreement is nearly zero because the implementers were present at its inception and took pains to see their own needs met in the process.

It is especially important in reaching and sustaining any close and associative relationship, that someone on each side be responsible for seeing that all promises are kept. It is absolutely critical to the quality of any long-term association that each party fully trusts that the other will do what they have said they would do. This applies between firms, between friends or between spouses. There is nothing more profound we could tell you about the art of persuasion than the fact that successful implementations breed future cooperation and reciprocal support.

For the selling organization, providing someone to keep the firm's overall response to the customer in reasonable alignment is normal practice because of the continual need to satisfy the customer. For the buying firm, this is an almost totally foreign approach. Buying organizations are traditionally reactive in nature. They react to someone else's determination of needs, or description of the crisis to be resolved, mostly as seen from the top internally. There is little opportunity to plan the requirements which stream in on them.

What we are recommending is a new posture which requires a very proactive approach from the buyer to their management and colleagues in order to get their involvement and gain their commitment to the prompt resolution of any problems which threaten this newly developed associative relationship. It will be especially necessary for buyers to guide the efforts of this mandate team to ensure that the supplier's needs are considered at the appropriate decision points (see Appendix I). The effort will be great, but the payback will be enormous as the customer firm finds itself able to motivate key suppliers to provide them with competitive advantages which the supplier will not offer to customers who do not make the same commitment to them.

The Reprographics Manufacturing Group of Xerox has carefully identified its *preferred* suppliers and greatly concentrated its substantial worldwide purchases with these firms. In the process, it reduced the supplier base from over 4000 firms to under 400.

As each new part is being developed, it is placed with one of these firms for the *life of the part*. In many cases, there is no competitive bidding, but rather Xerox and the chosen supplier jointly design a given part so it can be manufactured profitably within the cost Xerox can afford to incur, for the functioning of that part, and still be competitive with the best of their own world-class competitors (they call this process of measuring themselves against the best in the world "bench-marking" and have used it extensively in product design, manufacturing and marketing).

When competitive bids are indicated, they go only to other preferred suppliers, all of whom use statistical process control—often taught to them by Xerox—and who are known to have process capability equal to the high standards needed to remain in the much reduced supplier base. The criteria for being included in this supplier base are:

1 quality
2 design support capability and
3 cost

—in that order.

With purchased materials accounting for 80% of product costs, this approach was essential to their remarkable accomplishment—they reduced product cost by 50% in five years, simultaneously reducing days supply of working inventories by 75% and reducing supplier quality rejections by 80%.

It is more than a little significant that Xerox Reprographics is now saying that "long-term cooperative relationships with suppliers is a key strategy for success" and "Achieving competitive bench-mark targets, while maintaining fair and reasonable supplier profit margins, is essential to a healthy, long-term working relationship."

In the West, the very best firms are beginning to discover the power of such a commitment to their suppliers (see inset).

The necessarily close involvement of the negotiators with their internal mandate team provides a bountiful harvest of additional benefits for their companies and to those negotiators who in turn will be given greater authority and recognition. Negotiators who are confident of both their skills and their mandate do a better job for their firms than those who are to any significant degree uncertain or tentative.

Burt and Soukup (1985) provide us with a particularly clear example of the benefits of this close internal cooperation:

General Electric's jet engine division has carried the integration of engineering and purchasing to its logical conclusion and reaped significant cost and time savings. Some 16 design teams have worked on various aspects of GE's new commercial engine. Included on each team are three members of the materials (purchasing) organization: a procurement engineer, a buyer, and a subcontract administrator.

Vendors participate as appropriate throughout the design process. Normally, it takes three to four iterations through the design process to move from a clean sheet of paper on the drafting board to a workable product.

Although the final results are not yet in, GE estimates that its approach to product design will reduce the required iterations by 50% to 60% and prune costs by a whopping 20%!

The Risky Shift

"The Risky Shift" is a phrase we came across in our negotiation research and training, whose author we cannot trace, which aptly describes the phenomenon whereby a negotiator's confidence is such that he or she will be prepared to take a risk to get the deal they see possible—even if it means exceeding their mandate. Or they will refuse a deal which they see as damaging to their own side—even if it falls within their mandate—no matter what the pressure is to close. In short, the Risky Shift describes that extra bit of personal power the negotiator brings to the negotiation which can swing important deals.

Negotiators who are high on the Risky Shift are normally quicker to trust the other party, or to determine that they cannot be trusted, and act accordingly. Thus, to be a confident negotiator is something of a self-fulfilling prophecy, in which the confidence possessed encourages risks for progress, which bring greater success, which builds more confidence, which brings greater success, and so on.

So. it is very important for negotiators to go out with confidence when they represent their firm. But what can the organization do to enhance or maintain that confidence? The simple answer lies in the effective use of the mandate teams to underpin them. Confidence in negotiation comes with feeling that you know fairly certainly just what you can and cannot get your organization to accept and implement. Understanding its needs, those interests which underlie the "worst acceptable case" positions on each issue, gives the negotiator the basis for a quick, but accurate, assessment of every proposal which comes to the table. This allows that party to accept advantageous offers promptly, before they are withdrawn in a trade-off with something else, and to reject unacceptable offers without investing more time in them than they are worth.

This self-assurance also allows for accepting agreements somewhat outside the mandate limits on one point when an even greater advantage can thereby be obtained on another. This is possible because the negotiator is secure in the belief that they understand the true needs of the mandate team members, who will therefore support the favorable trade-off they have engineered. And if the deviation from the mandate is great enough to give pause, they know precisely what must be done—counsel with the mandate team itself to assess their willingness to implement an agreement at the value being offered.

All this constitutes an essential first step in preparing to deal with the underlying interests of all parties to this associative relationship we are recommending, and provides a working definition of win–win. The supplier's overall perception of the customer firm—and therefore their responsiveness to its needs—will grow out of their cumulative experience at the many points where they touch the customer's organization (touch-points). The customer firm that incorporates this single fact into its strategies will be much more likely to manage all of those touch points to their mutual long-term advantage. The conscious managing of perceptions and relationships is called "touch-point management," and here is an introduction to one aspect of it.

TOUCH-POINT MANAGEMENT

For the firm who has decided that it needs to give consistent preferential problem-solving treatment to its preferred suppliers, in order to enjoy preferential treatment *from them* in return, there is a logical way to approach the process. First they must identify the touch-points by laying out the specific decisions and the ongoing processes which impact the functional relationships involved. Let us take, for example, the relationships around an engineering function. The specifications for materials for a given component constitute a specific decision at the part-number level, which will affect the engineering relationship between customer and supplier in some way. The customer firm's process for dealing with production changes initiated in the field is an example of an ongoing process, which also can impact the engineering relationship between customer and supplier. For any given component, material or service being supplied from inside or outside the customer firm, it is possible to identify these item-specific decisions and ongoing processes. Having done this, it is then possible to lay them out in a way which produces a map of those touch-points which are important to that buyer–seller relationship. Figure 6.5, an example of a typical manufacturing component, illustrates this.

The diagonal lines indicate which relationships are being impacted by each item-specific decision listed above, and the small circles indicate which are being impacted by the ongoing processes listed below. In this typical example, there are 20 touch-points created by the item-specific decisions, e.g. prototype sourcing impacts product engineering, purchasing, material control and manufacturing. There are 23 touch-points created by the ongoing processes. In eight cases, the impact at that touch-point can come from either direction or both. Both the original design and later product update from the field can impact production, engineering, purchasing, quality, manufacturing and finance (see Figure 6.6).

The explicit identification of these touch-points provides a guide for managing the relationship processes not totally unlike statistical process control for manufacturing operations. It should be possible to determine when that touch-point is "in control" and when it is "out of control" and when it is moving in one direction or the other. For a given commodity being purchased, it should be possible to name the manager responsible for each touch-point. They will also be prime candidates for mandate team membership to the degree they own that piece of the act.

Continuing with the example, if you accept that the ability of this customer firm to influence the supplier of that item to provide preferential treatment is shaped by the supplier's cumulative perception of that customer's willingness to help that supplier meet their needs, then it follows that the supplier's perception of that willingness is the thing needing to be measured and kept "in control." This forms a kind of X-bar-R Chart if done properly. And the proper way to find out if each touch-point is "in control" in the suppliers perception is to ask the supplier in a manner sufficiently probing to allow suitable analysis.

A set of questions can be developed to probe the features which are important at each touch-point in the eyes of the supplier. You should then ask those questions of the people whose views matter—the members of the supplier side of those touch-points whose collective assessment will determine

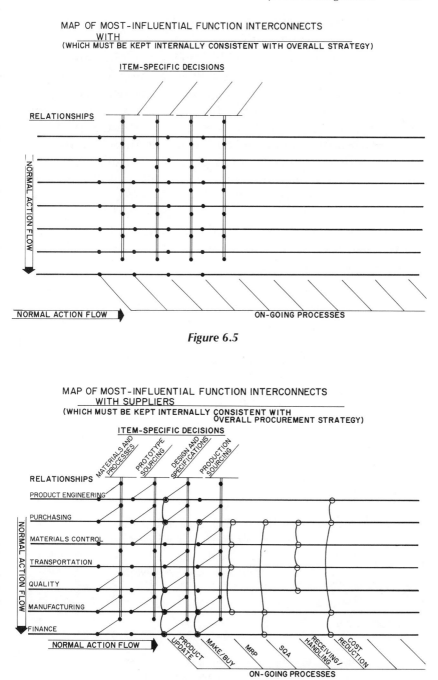

MAP OF MOST-INFLUENTIAL FUNCTION INTERCONNECTS
WITH
(WHICH MUST BE KEPT INTERNALLY CONSISTENT WITH OVERALL STRATEGY)

ITEM-SPECIFIC DECISIONS

RELATIONSHIPS

NORMAL ACTION FLOW

NORMAL ACTION FLOW ▶   ON-GOING PROCESSES

Figure 6.5

MAP OF MOST-INFLUENTIAL FUNCTION INTERCONNECTS
WITH SUPPLIERS
(WHICH MUST BE KEPT INTERNALLY CONSISTENT WITH
OVERALL PROCUREMENT STRATEGY)

ITEM-SPECIFIC DECISIONS

MATERIALS AND PROCESSES
PROTOTYPE SOURCING
DESIGN AND SPECIFICATIONS
PRODUCTION SOURCING

RELATIONSHIPS

PRODUCT ENGINEERING

PURCHASING

MATERIALS CONTROL

TRANSPORTATION

QUALITY

MANUFACTURING

FINANCE

NORMAL ACTION FLOW

NORMAL ACTION FLOW ▶

PRODUCT UPDATE
MAKE/BUY
MRP
SQA
RECEIVING/HANDLING
COST REDUCTION

ON-GOING PROCESSES

Figure 6.6

the level of preferential treatment to be given. This identifies for customer management those touch-points which are being managed more in keeping with a policy of giving preferential problem-solving treatment to preferred suppliers and those which are not. By asking for a current assessment and also for the assessment which would have prevailed at some earlier point, it is also possible to determine which touch-points are moving towards "out of control." It should then be possible to identify those touch-point managers whose exemplary rating suggests that they should be mentoring others to improve the overall assessment level. The following extract from a questionnaire gives some typical questions which would elicit assessments sufficiently focused and sufficiently detailed to allow such analysis of the important influences on the relationship under scrutiny.

CONFIDENTIAL SURVEY QUESTIONNAIRE FOR KEY SUPPLIERS

A   Item-specific interconnects

   I   *Materials and processes*
        (a) Relative to your present typical customer, are the functions you contact at (_____) more receptive or less receptive to considering your ideas and suggestions for incorporating lower-cost materials and processes into the products you supply us?

	Much more receptive		Average		Much less receptive	
Product engineering	7	6	5	4	3	2	1
Purchasing	7	6	5	4	3	2	1
Quality	7	6	5	4	3	2	1
Manufacturing	7	6	5	4	3	2	1
Finance	7	6	5	4	3	2	1

        (b) Had we asked the above question five years ago, how would have you rated the listed (_____) function at that time?

	Much more receptive		Average		Much less receptive	
Product engineering	7	6	5	4	3	2	1
Purchasing	7	6	5	4	3	2	1
Quality	7	6	5	4	3	2	1
Manufacturing	7	6	5	4	3	2	1
Finance	7	6	5	4	3	2	1

        (c) Relative to your present typical customer, are the functions you contact at (_____) faster or slower to respond?

. . . and so on.

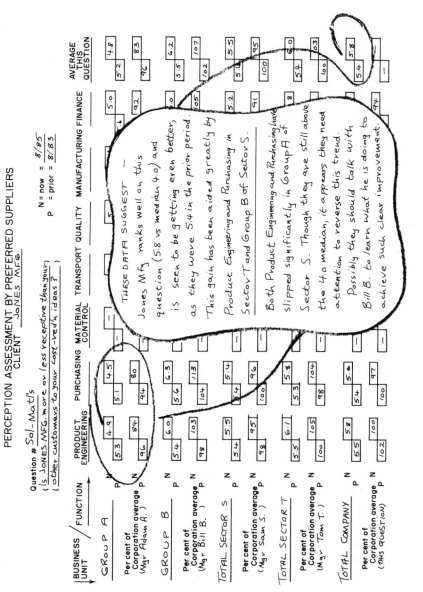

Figure 6.7

For firms using this approach, there is another possibility— that of determining which touch-point managers are aware of their problems (and therefore most likely to be addressing them) and which are unaware of their problems, in their outside relationships. This is done simply by asking the touch-point managers the same questions to be asked of the suppliers, but requesting them to advise the rating that they *expect* to receive from the preferred suppliers on each question. Those who predict a low rating and receive it, are aware of, and probably working on, the problem. Those who predict a high rating and receive it, are possibly the best candidates as mentors, because they very likely know what they are doing well. Those who predict a significantly higher rating than they receive may well have problems of which they are unaware, and therefore, most likely need help, possibly from those who are doing pretty well where that manager is not.

This concept can be worked in both directions, of course, because both buyer and seller can identify their touch-point managers, and further specify which of them are members of their mandate team for that commodity or item. This becomes an exercise in consciousness-raising about the human processes which link organizations, and thereby puts the "heart" back into the buyer–seller transaction by recognizing the relationships and attitudes which are important on both sides.

This approach provides a reasonably comfortable forum for explicitly addressing any practice or behavior which is seen from the assessment to be causing particular stress. Such things are too often seen as sensitive matters because of their judgmental nature. Somehow the very fact of treating them in this more objective manner seems to remove some of their threat and replace it with more purposeful consideration of what now becomes an observable problem which needs corrective action. Good managers usually want to know how they are performing against valid outside measures. This process can give them a yardstick and a forum for improvement.

Mandate teams who have reached a high level of integration and mutual support become increasingly candid with each other without so much fear of precipitating unpleasant personal reactions. This allows them to address such an assessment of themselves by outsiders in a more nearly dispassionate but keenly interested way. This empathetic approach provides both a relationship review of considerable value and a spur to encourage them to work directly and explicitly on the relationships in question. This leads to a passion for truth—which is the first platform for real performance-development ideas.

The bad news is that mandate teams are slow to reach this state of "intimacy," in which each member will risk becoming open with the others in the belief that they will not take undue advantage of that openness. But there is good news too, and that is that the process can be accelerated. And what follows in the remaining chapters is a process for deliberately and consciously advancing multidiscipline groups, such as mandate teams, towards the level of candid exchange required to use touch-point management to its fullest potential.

Mandate teams and the touch-point management approach will then be posited as a means for resolving issues as they arise in a way which builds a mutually beneficial interdependence between buyer and seller

DEVELOPING THE COMMON GROUND

Issues, problems and differences of opinion will continue to arise in any important relationship, be it a marriage, a business partnership or a group of working colleagues. If the relationship is built on a foundation of substantial common ground involving shared goals and interests, these differences will be less frequent than otherwise, but not totally absent. Even in the most durable and supportive of relationships, differences will arise simply because both parties will continue primarily to address their own needs and interests, which will not always coincide neatly with the needs and interests of the other party.

In the buyer–seller relationship, particularly, there is the constant danger that either party may sense an opportunity to enhance their own benefits substantially by ignoring the needs of the other party regarding a specific transaction (win–lose). If that transaction is seen as an event within an ongoing relationship, it is essential that both parties search for ways to resolve the issue in question in a way which both can view as satisfactory (win–win).

When all is said and done, then, the working definition of a win–win agreement between buyer and seller, which emerges from all this, is one in which the positions of both parties on all issues have been resolved in a way in which buyer and seller mandate teams will want to implement the agreement.

This dictates that the external negotiation is not finished until the partners have addressed the impact of the proposed resolution of each issue on the relationship itself. This is best done by the negotiators satisfying themselves, by whatever means are required, that their own mandate teams want to implement the agreed resolution of every issue in all particulars. The very process of testing the proposed agreement against both sides' mandate team's needs, will produce the opportunity to resolve any remaining differences in position, by addressing the real needs of those most vitally concerned. This enables the negotiators to get past any difficult positions in order to reach their partner's real interests, as is so eloquently demanded by Ury and Fisher. And it strengthens the foundation under the relationship by ensuring that all touch-points between "the partners" form a circle of support for it.

Finally, by jointly working to assure that both mandate teams are satisfied, this strategy makes full use of Axelrod's penetrating insight that sustained cooperation grows exclusively where sustained cooperation is anticipated in return.

The development and use of mandate teams in the above manner establishes a macro-strategy for resolving internal functional differences. It accomplishes this in a way which encourages consistent behavior by all disciplines in providing preferential problem-solving to selected outsiders from whom you want preferential treatment in return. This puts the heart back into the special relationships involved and assures that needs and attitudes will be considered and dealt with all around.

By following the above-described process you are ready to identify and develop mandate teams, primarily to resolve internal differences and promote consistent effort on a common and uniform front. The next step is to provide those mandate teams with the conditions for coordinated external action which will attract the competitive advantage desired. That is the substance of the next chapter.

SELECTED REFERENCES

Burt, D. and Soukup, R. "Purchasing's Role in New Product Development," *Harvard Business Review*, September–October, pp. 90–97 (1985).

Harvard Business Review, Editorial, January–February (1985).

Kanter, R. M. *The Change Masters*. Counterpoint, London (1985).

7
Creating the Right Conditions

And suffer not the barren-handed to take part in your transactions,
who would sell their words for your labour.

(Kahlil Gibran: The Prophet)

In the preceding six chapters it has been our intention to establish the following points.

- interdependent relationships in industrial buying and selling can create handsome benefits
- cooperation is the best strategy for developing these relationships
- the opportunity for competitive advantage is *now*
- new players with cooperative buyer–seller relationships are taking away our customers
- buyer–seller interdependence offers the best unexplored opportunity for gaining competitive advantage but
- there are many personal forces working against good buyer–seller relationships and
- there are many organizational forces working against good buyer–seller relationships
- the Mandate Team *is* the solution to this puzzle.

Now we must create the blueprint for turning interdependence to our own advantage, the first part of which is a simp-

Focus on:
The customer
and supplier
quality
relationship

{

The Executive
Responsible for
creating the *vision*
for the future, and
the *conditions* for
success.

The management
Responsible for
continuous
improvement of the
systems that bring
people and resources
together more
effectively.

The Workers
Responsible for
doing the best
possible job, given
the vision, and
systems prevailing.

lified, but useful, model of looking at who is responsible for what in an organization.

The challenge for this chapter, then, is to light the way in the search for that common ground between buyer and seller from which mutual advantage can best spring. And by common ground we mean that territory bounded by those conditions both parties would like to see exist *for their own separate reasons,* or defined by those events both parties would like to see occur—*also for their own separate reasons.* In a nutshell, this chapter should help the reader determine what to do next in his or her own personal search for this common ground.

THE MANDATE TEAM IS THE FIRST STEP

That organizations can really get in the way of effective business relationships is not a reason for despair. Such a reaction would only be warranted if the organization had no impact at all on the quality of relationships.

The ability that organizations have to cause damage is only one side of the spectrum of their purpose. They also have the ability to enrich lives, to provide a climate for profitable and useful activities—if they are balanced and aligned. Those very principles of structure and function which can cripple relationships are exactly the same as those which involve people effectively and liberate their talents.

The mandate team, as a mini-organization for development in *both* buying and supplying organizations, can provide the balance and alignment that the buyer–supplier relationship demands. It cannot operate in a vacuum; thus certain conditions must be provided by the leaders in the organization before it will really become effective.

CREATING THE RIGHT INTERNAL CONDITIONS

1   Vision

A sense of purpose has to be displayed through a clear mission statement. John Sculley, CEO of Apple, said: "The new age leaders will lead not with toughness but with powerful ideas" (Sculley and Byrne, 1987). This clarity can only come from an executive that has worked through very clearly what this *idea* is, i.e. of the nature of purchasing in the organization. Xerox, Motorola, Tektronix, Ford and Chrysler are typical of the companies who have made public their vision for purchasing–vendor relationships. Gerald Greenwald, Chairman of Chrysler Motors said that the new goals for the office of procurement and supply are: zero defects, 100% just-in-time delivery from suppliers, control of commodity prices, participation in the company's 30% per unit cost-cutting program, and a continuation of sound long-term relationships with the suppliers (*Purchasing*, 1987). Chrysler are even creating the physical embodiment of their vision in the Supplier Office Park site, which will take up 65 acres of the 503 acre Chrysler Technology Center. This is really working it through! And this has been recognized by their being awarded the 1987 Medal of Professional Excellence by *Purchasing* magazine.

Every executive who intends to change purchasing policy, fundamentally needs first to exercise the creativity of everyone in purchasing, by considering their views and taking into account the picture of the future they would like. They then need to exercise their own imagination in a bold way, which does not just replicate the past with some hitech knobs on it. And they must be courageous enough to publish their vision in such a way that everyone in the company knows that there is a new objective which is realistic and meaningful, and not just another "flavor of the month" illusion. However, before any of this can happen, a fundamental activity must take place—and incur activity. Top management must look regularly at themselves and ask: "How capable are we of delivering this?" No organizational change will work *without the people at the top also changing*. This is axiomatic, and yet it is ignored time and again, as major change ideas frequently emanate *from* the top whilst often only minor change, if any, occurs *at* the top.

2 Ethics

The way an organization behaves as a whole is a reflection of the conscious versus unconscious orientation of the top layer of management. Putting aside the truly immoral behavior of some of the more iconoclastic participants in the Stock Market revolution, companies need, nevertheless, to look at their own practices.

It has not just been the Lockheeds and the Toshibas of this world who have been guilty of serious misconduct getting business in the past: malpractice exists in many different forms. Sometimes it occurs because the suppliers are inefficient and unprofessional, and use bribes to get business they do not deserve—instead of using that money to invest in their own operation to improve it. This is only slightly worse than spending millions of dollars on marketing to push a product which simply is not good enough, instead of investing in modifying it to really meet consumer needs. Sudden rushes of advertising and promotion ought to make us anxious about the quality and utility of a particular product. At other times, business may go to the organization which does deserve it on pure merit, but which perceives that they will not get it without greasing palms. This attempt at bribery seriously offends the ethical buyer, and can damage the relationship irreparably.

All this demonstrates a lack of respect for other people in organizations in the manufacturing chain, a morality distorted by rationalization, and, most damagingly for both parties, a lack of service consciousness towards the end user who, after all, is the final arbiter of their fate. An example of moral leadership was quoted admiringly by a businessman at one of the Conference Board Meetings in 1975 (a respected United States business institute which holds off-the-record meetings for business leaders): "The highest code is something like that expressed by Erwin Miller of Cummins Engine who called his top management together, after the American Airlines illegal contribution was disclosed, to reiterate his policy of '100% adherence to 100% honesty, even if we lose by it' . . ." (Silk and Vogel, 1976).

Ross Perot is another outstanding example of someone who makes a corporate policy on ethics actually work. In EDS's code of conduct it is written:

> A determination that a payment or practice is not forbidden by law does not conclude the analysis . . . it is always appropriate to make further inquiry into ethics . . . could you do business in complete trust with someone who acts the way you do? The answer must be YES. . . .
>
> If you have to pay bribes to do business there [in Iran], why, we just won't do business there.
>
> (Follett, 1983)

This constitutes a modern version of another Kantian view: "If you would determine the appropriateness of an act, think not of the consequences of the act itself, but of the consequences if everyone were to proceed as you now propose to do."

Perot and Miller's way may not only be more ethical, it also makes better business sense. When it comes to immoral behavior that may benefit the corporation, such as payoffs, there is a lot of truth in the street wisdom that once you start to pay, all you can do is pay more. Gulf made payoffs of close to $500,000 to the President of Bolivia to prevent expropriations by a repressive regime. After the bribe was disclosed, the new regime said it would withhold over $5,000,000 still due to Gulf in indemnity.

In the notorious Lockheed scandal of the 1970s, which precipitated a tidal wave of regulations and investigations, the large bribe given by Lockheed to the Tanaka government in Japan was partly used to persuade All-Nippon Airways *not* to buy the Lockheed Tri-Star. And, most recently, the Ernest Saunders affair has really damaged the image of what was a highly regarded company—Guinness.

To quote Peter Drucker (1982) again:

> Business ethics means that one side has obligations and the other side has rights, if not entitlements. This one-sidedness is not compatible with the ethics of interdependence and indeed with any ethics at all. It is the politics of power, and indeed the politics of naked exploitation and repression. And within the context of interdependence the exploiters and the oppressors are not the bosses but the ones who assert their rights rather than accept mutual obligation and with it, equality.

3   Resources

Top management commitments to a change in policy must be made visible. The three components of visibility are:

1   A clear plan and a development budget. If these are not published (see the Chrysler example above), then do not expect the new policy to be taken seriously.
2   Time must be made available for the new initiatives.
3   Interest has to be displayed by the executive consciously and with a proper process, both before and after the change initiative. A very important part of this is the communication process. Very often in its need to make sure that the marketplace and shareholders know what the new aspirations are, and that the suppliers are made aware of the planned preferred supplier approach (the external communications), so much the company not forget to get the *internal* communications right. This point is emphasized by Jim Sierk, who guided the very successful supplier reduction effort at Xerox, in a very thoughtful response to an

early draft of this work that Bob sent to him. He wrote: "it is essential that a large-scale massive communication program occurs up front . . . The CEO has to be part of that process."

4   Performance appraisal

Management will need to see that there are new norms in place, and know that their own performance will be judged on this. Too often they are put in a double bind by their executives, who demand that new policies be carried out, but then continue to reward or punish on the old criteria. For example, in General Motors it is still being reported in some plants that meeting the production schedules comes first, even though quality is proclaimed to be the top priority. This really unsettles the supervisors. On the other hand, Ford rewards managers for teamwork.

THE VISION MADE VISIBLE

So, having pulled the development group together around the vision, and with the appropriate conditions, the next step in coming to be perceived by suppliers as willing to help them meet their needs, lies quite simply in using the mandate team to understand what those needs truly are. Again, this is easier in organizations at the pioneer phase, but much harder to determine in organizations which are in the rational/scientific phase—hence the need for the mandate team. Managers within such organizations often find it difficult to describe their firm's true needs because of the way the structure lowers their consciousness, so it is no wonder that outsiders buying from or selling to them find it near impossible to describe their needs.

For the customer firm wishing to influence key suppliers it is doubly important to keep trying. Just as quality guru Phil Crosby says that "zero defects" is more a journey than a destination, so must the buying firm keep seeking an ever-better understanding of the needs of key suppliers in order to maintain continuous improvement. Happily, the very process of seeking actively to understand the supplier's true needs will give off very clear signals to the supplier that the buyer is at least interested in those needs—and nothing is more likely to begin to reduce uncertainty and to begin to induce cooperative behavior. This also applies when searching out customer needs, as every skilled salesperson knows.

This kind of inner-directed search by the customer firm to understand the selling party's needs will only occur if the customer firm believes, at the general management level, that such behavior is in their own interests. They must understand this point so well that they will invest in resources and the organization to make it happen, as there is no better way to illustrate strength of purpose than by letting "justice be seen to be done,"especially in a complex relationship involving multiple functions on both sides. It is also true that any deliberate attempt to "appear" to be interested in the other party's needs is foredoomed to failure because (a) deception, even by default, is simply not the right way to do business, and (b) no one has a memory good enough to be a successful liar for very long. So, justice will be seen to be done only if both sides' needs are met and the opportunities developed together. Let us examine how and why.

CREATING THE RIGHT CONDITIONS FOR SUPPLIERS

To repeat, we feel that the initiative for developing the buyer–seller relationship must be taken by the buying firm. The customer firm must explicitly provide for the meeting of all needs which the supplier can legitimately expect, and they must train and/or motivate all their personnel involved to treat these needs seriously and to deal with them as promptly as they would their own firm's.

1   Offer Early Involvement—it Pays

The supplier must have access to product design as early as humanly possible in the design process to assure optimal use of any special skills or processes they can contribute. For specially designed products, the epitome of this would mean placing the production business by means of direct negotiation before prototype development.

At the IBM plant in Boulder, Colorado, which produces sophisticated disk drives and other products, it was determined that, as part of an overall program to instil pride in all phases of the operation and its products, the very best component sources should be identified and sourced with newly conceived parts before the end product was fully designed. This would allow maximum opportunity for including the supplier's best ideas in the final product, be they feature ideas, process ideas, or be they aimed at cost reduction or product improvement, all of which will tend to improve the likelihood that "their" product will land the consumer sale.

This naturally required several steps quite foreign to the traditional market determined placement of this production business:

(a) The customer had to decide precisely which supplier was a "world-class" best for each component. This required a new form of soul-searching—and evaluation of the longer-term aspects of their relationships with the candidate suppliers. It also demanded something unusual—that they trust their own judgment in reaching these conclusions without letting the market help them.

(b) The customer had to develop a very clear picture of how much they were willing to pay for components sourced this way—and remember that the components in question had not been designed yet. This was accomplished by having product engineering produce a conceptual sketch which identified parameters, such as envelope, attachment, inputs and outputs. Then assumptions were made regarding materials and processes sufficient to establish an estimate of the most-likely cost on the competitive market for such components.

(c) The customer then had to negotiate the placement of their production volume requirements on a permanent basis, without any test of the price the open market would place on such a component. It is little wonder that the customer's buyers were often the ones who most resisted this bizarre approach to industrial buying. It deprived them of their customary feel for the market, and it forced them to trust their own judgment, both in selecting the "best" source, and in negotiating a resolution of many commercial issues, including price, after declaring that they wanted to place the business with this particular supplier.

The payout of this associative approach to sourcing lies in the fact that advantageous product and process ideas of the suppliers are being incorporated at the outset, rather than later, or never, depending on the difficulty of later changing the product to incorporate these ideas. And the delivered cost of new components sourced in this collaborative fashion are costing IBM 7–10% less than their most aggressive internal estimates. This type of success is being repeated in a number of the more thoughtful firms around the world (not just in Japan) and is the reward for what is basically an act of faith.

2   Be Prepared to Play an Occasional Red (I Can Reward You)

Product design and manufacturing process must be open to modification where there is a benefit to be gained, even when the immediate benefit is only to the supplier. Here is a prime opportunity to follow the advice of Confucius by enhancing the benefit (to the supplier) of this important interdependency, rather than acting only when there is a clear and present benefit to yourself within that action. Here the mandate team can play an important strategic role in this effort because it can provide the forum within which such considerations can be weighed. It is in the best position to make an informed evaluation of any potential risks or costs, and to judge whether or not they should be undertaken purely to support the special relationship involved. For example, the mandate team could decide whether to design a manufacturing enabler into a component which would ease a supplier problem, but would not produce a cost-reduction. This would be a clear relationship-enhancement decision.

3   Consider the Implications for your Supplier

Schedule and delivery requirement processes should interact with the supplier before customer production decisions are made, to ensure that benefits accruing to both parties collectively are properly compared with the costs to both parties collectively—before taking action. Because the natural inclination of the customer firm is to look after their own needs first, and maybe only, there is a predisposition to adjust the production schedule to meet a customer or market change without considering the impact on suppliers. The only natural limit to this is the physical limit to the supplier's ability to respond in time. The costs generated within the supplier to support these abrupt schedule changes are far too often ignored by the customer operation—if they can get away with it. In the short term, then, the customer has managed to meet their own needs by doing great violence to the needs of the supplier. Too often, the customer firm acts a bit like Hagar the Horrible in the cartoon below.

(reproduced by permission of Yaffa)

But, as we observed before, those "costs of violence" must find their way into the price paid by the customer firm, and ultimately into the price asked of the real consumer. Enlightened customer firms recognize this, and endeavor, out of their own long-term interests, to ask their key suppliers to advise more than simply whether or not they can physically manage to perform the newly desired schedule. They endeavor in some way to include the disruption and cost impacts on their suppliers in the original decision regarding how best to accommodate the given customer or market development. The supplier's preferences will not always prevail, but at least in these more progressive firms, the supplier has been heard and their needs considered in the decision process. They can thus better accept any disappointment which may follow, knowing that their customer firm was considering both sets of needs in attempting to satisfy the final consumer. This kind of preventive maintenance, performed on the relationship itself, is a prime responsibility of the "world-class" buyer.

4   Solve Problems Together

Supplier problems must be seen as joint responsibilities and resolved just as quickly as problems of the customer's own manufacturing operations would be resolved. This requires that resources of both the buyer and seller be brought to bear on "our" problems in a way which produces the most efficient use of "our" resources—that is, the collective resources of both parties. This follows the "greater good for the greater number" idea, where the two parties collectively represent the greater number. In some manufacturing chains it should be possible to extend this idea upstream towards Mother Earth and downstream towards the consumer—always with the intention of increasing the likelihood that the consumer will choose "our" product and thereby reward all of "us."

In the Communications Sector of Motorola, which is pursuing a program to achieve an associative relationship with its key suppliers, an interesting body has been established to guide the effort. This body is called the "Partners for Growth Advisory Board," and consists of general management from 15 key suppliers, ten Motorola general managers, and ten Motorola purchasing managers.

At an early meeting, these 35 advisory board members brainstormed a number of questions regarding the relationship between all key suppliers (about 400) and Motorola, such as "how can Motorola break down any remaining obstacles to the partnership feeling we desire between suppliers and ourselves?" The answers tended to focus on suggestions, such as "get key suppliers involved in early design development" and "establish preferred suppliers (loyalty, trust, qualified, etc.)." After brainstorming several questions separately and collectively and producing some 160 ideas, each member determined what they considered to be the top ten in each category. These votes were aggregated in descending order, thus identifying the ten most appealing ideas in the collective view of all 35 members. The focus question was "what can you suggest Motorola do which would cause key suppliers to want to do things for Motorola which they don't do for their other customers." Those who are inclined to be cynical about the behavior of suppliers when they have the opportunity to influence the policies of the key customer (as this board does) might expect the No. 1 rating to go to "allow higher profits"—which in fact came in dead last; or "progress payments on product/programs" which came in 43rd out of 48 on this question. Instead, the action deemed most likely to cause suppliers to want to do things for Motorola which they don't do for their other customers turned out to be:

"give preferential problem-solving to preferred suppliers in:

—payables   —inventory
—engineering   —schedule
—quality   —any problem they raise."

In the Motorola example above, the general managers of those "best" supplier firms, in each of the 15 most significant commodities, were saying that the behavior which would most motivate them to give preferential treatment to a customer was that customer's extension of preferential treatment to them whenever they raised a problem at any of the touch-points between the two firms. Or to repeat once again that most profound insight, they were affirming that any customer's ability to influence them was largely determined by their perception of that customer's willingness to help them meet their own needs.

5   Fairness Pays Off in the Longer Term

Supplier margins must be considered in the original and in the ongoing agreement on pricing. It is productive (and fair to the other parties in the manufacturing chain) to expect all supplier margins to be slim when the marketplace demands, so long as all supplier margins are allowed to recover when the opportunity exists. There is no long-term advantage to any customer in the chain from keeping their supplier margins below a level which meets the supplier's investment/return needs. Xerox Reprographics considers this a key element in their long-term strategy (as outlined in Chapter 4).

6   Keep the Key Players in the Picture

The key suppliers must have knowledge of coming events which could affect their contribution to this associative relationship in any way—or which could affect the meeting of any of their now recognized needs. In short, the key suppliers must be treated as though they were important manufacturing departments of the customer firm. This is likely to happen only if the buyer is clearly accountable for managing the relationship, sufficiently aware of the need to communicate, has the skills to do so, and is plugged into coming events through the mandate team.

7   Develop Opportunities Together

The final step for the customer firm which wants to be perceived as interested in the needs of key suppliers, is to create specific and explicit mechanisms for drawing out supplier contributions in product design, manufacturing processes, quality/reliability and communications processes between all related functions. The creating and leadership of these mechanisms should normally fall to the responsible buyer with management support from all disciplines he or she needs to involve.

(a) Value analysis and value engineering are good beginning steps, but probably not as full-time departments. It is usually more productive to establish *ad hoc* structures, temporarily involving the actual decision-makers, while addressing the commodities they control. This is another ideal use of the mandate team which, after all, is composed of the people who know the target commodity best. The supplier should usually create a mirror structure of decision-makers at their end, with their sales representatives responsible for its creation and leadership.

(b) Technology-sharing can be especially productive where both parties feel fully committed to a long-term associative relationship. Given the premise that all costs reach the customer, it is counterproductive to expect a second party in the manufacturing chain to consume resources in developing or adapting an emerging product or process technology, if anyone else in that chain could pass it over to them at less cost to the whole chain (again, Confucian interdependence at its best).

(c) Supplier ideas should be rewarded and specifically encouraged by allowing them, at least temporarily, a wider than usual share of margins wherever their ideas create a better benefit to any one in the chain (sometimes the benefit accrues a step or two later in the chain). Nothing sparks creativity better than prompt recognition and a visible, valuable reward. This may well represent the corporate equivalent to the individual's prime need for recognition of self-worth as identified by Alderfer.

For some years Ford Motor Company has operated a program to encourage new productivity and cost-reduction proposals from machinery and tooling suppliers. In essence, any idea submitted by a supplier is circulated to ensure that it does not duplicate any other under study. When seen as truly new and unique, the proposal is assigned a serial number and pursued for feasibility. There is no attempt to negotiate the prices put forward for any machinery or tooling in the proposal needed to implement the idea. It is understood that Ford will buy that machinery or tooling only from the firm who originated the proposal, and at the price requested, if the equipment to be purchased generates savings sufficient to meet the hurdle of Ford's internal return-on-investment rate. This concept has produced many equipment purchases without competitive bidding and has brought forth many cost-reduction ideas Ford would not otherwise have enjoyed.

In one case, a supplier of precision stamping dies noticed a problem Ford was having with a gear assembly encased in a die casting. He proposed that it be redesigned as a stamped assembly, but Ford engineers were doubtful of the durability of such an agreement. Being confident that Ford would buy the necessary tooling from him at his price if it proved feasible and profitable, the supplier built up an expensive set of tools at his own cost and made up several samples for engineering to test. The samples proved his point and Ford bought the production tooling from him at a price well above normal. Even at the inflated price, the savings to Ford were well within their return-on-investment hurdle rate and this was an idea they would not otherwise have had at all. Truly a win—win conclusion, based on the suppliers perception that Ford would be willing to meet their needs.

A history of mutually satisfactory experiences such as the above helped. Ford developed the Simultaneous Engineering approach to capital equipment purchasing which can shorten the tooling cycle for a new model by as much as a year (see Appendix II).

In summary, the supplier should increasingly be seen as a voluntary member of the customer family. The buyers, then, should be seen as a prime resource to the supplier with responsibility for ensuring that all customer disciplines can and do play their part to cause this associative relationship to recognize and deal with the needs of both parties. The buyer also must be seen by all other customer disciplines (mandate team members) as responsible for ensuring that the supplier continues to meet their needs—and should have a say in determining which suppliers will be designated as "preferred." The rights, privileges and responsibilities which accrue to the supplier in the associative relationship, are in many ways mirror images of the same rights, privileges and responsibilities which exist on the customer side. This is by no means a soft or generous condition we are describing. It is rather one in which both sides vigorously pursue their own interests, but in a mutually supportive way which at times makes two plus two equal more than four.

The posture we urge both buyer and seller firms to adopt is, in fact, quite self-interested because it is the posture which has been shown to lead to the greatest benefit for the firm adopting it, given a sufficiently long-term view and consistent behavior. Buyer and seller were not among the five prime inter-dependencies seen by Confucius in the simpler times of 500 BC, but they would surely qualify in today's much more complex and interconnected world. Bear in mind that Con-fucius said both parties would do well to strive to enhance the benefit of the interdependence, rather than striving to enhance their own share of that benefit. This is another way of saying that, interdependence, if viewed positively, will lead to a beneficial creativity—rather than the divided spoils that is all that can be expected from a self-protective stance.

The firm that accepts the role of preferred supplier under-takes to earn preferential treatment by taking their best efforts and most valuable ideas to that preferred customer *first*. Coop-eration blossoms where cooperation is reciprocated. So the supplier must take risks and make equal efforts along with their customer for that associative relationship to emerge; this chapter has been about creating the conditions which nurture risk-taking and creative goodwill.

In the next chapter, we look at the many barriers to the initiation and sustaining of that relationship, and at the ways these can be anticipated: this is the micro-strategy.

SELECTED REFERENCES

Drucker, P. *The Changing World of the Executive*. Heinemann, London (1982).

Follett, K. *On the Wings of Eagles*. William Morrow, New York (1983).

Purchasing, "Medal of Professional Excellence Award" to Chrysler, July 16 (1987).

Sculley, J. and Byrne, J. *Odyssey . . . a Journey of Adventure. Ideas and the Future*. Harper & Row, New York (1987).

Silk, L. and Vogel, D. *Ethics and Profits*. Simon & Schuster, New York (1976).

8
Letting Go the Rock

American Managers, as a group need to reduce their pulse rate . . .
They need to drink in their organisational experience and discover
more deeply what makes things work. From that wisdom can come,
which is, in the end, perhaps the greatest reward from a life of
managerial work, and the quality most needed for organisations to
become great ones.

(Pascale and Athos, 1982)

This chapter is directed at the management within the buying
organization because they are the ones who need to take the
initiative in changing the old habits and setting the new styles
and systems. And because they are the people who can deliver
the micro-strategy by creating the conditions for the new relationships to be executed at the inferface of individual buyer and
supplier. They are the ones who can "play a Red" (see the
Red–Blue exercise, Chapter 4), because they have the power.

It is meant to be both a cautionary and encouraging chapter:
cautionary because buyers do not have a good reputation by
and large; encouraging because careful, thoughtful, strategies
can overcome this, as Xerox in particular has demonstrated, to
the extent that they were awarded the annual *Purchasing* magazine Medal of Professional Excellence for the outstanding progress of their materials management with suppliers within the
Reprographic Manufacturing Group (1985).

"Letting go the rock" was the statement used by the now
beleaguered Roger Smith, CEO of General Motors shortly after
he assumed that position. It evokes a powerful image, meaning
as it did to let go the old familiar, and no longer effective, habits
in order to take up the new, unfamiliar, but survival-dependent

136

ways of managing. However, stirring words are not sufficient a spur to action when major change is required. The General Motors situation demonstrates this—as does Austin Rover (British Leyland), the old Woolworths, USX, etc. In effect, the list comprises those very industries which prompted Tom Peters controversially to extol the functional necessity of corporate raiders for the development of company productivity and ultimate survival. Exhortations and slogans do not really work—as Deming keeps telling us.

So, what does work? Simply this: turning the idea of the effective supplier relationships into the reality of these relationships depends totally on the executive *not* playing intellectual games with the theory but, instead, embodying it in visionary leadership and effective policy—as the previous chapter attempts to demonstrate. The next step is to look at the role of management in translating it into good practice, both inside and outside the corporation. This requires the microstrategy, the positioning of the most effective interfaces between the internal and external working groups in the purchasing relationship. It means thinking carefully and consciously about innovative social and technical systems for bringing about and sustaining the new relationships needed. This chapter is about the issues, implications of the strategy—and the payoff, when followed through with commitment.

OBSTACLES IN THE WAY OF CHANGING RELATIONSHIPS

Helping people let go their rock and work in new ways is the major challenge to management today. In the buyer–supplier relationship it is the crucial challenge. It means going beyond just talking about the policies for mandate groups and going public on "preferred supplier" strategies. It means setting up effective social and technological systems to replace those which keep suppliers at bay, because just removing barriers does not change behavior. Take, for example, an anecdote by Konrad Lorenz, the famous animal behaviorist, which can be extended quite easily to people.

Lorenz had a small terrier which he took for a walk every day past a neighbor's house. The neighbor also had a terrier and the two dogs appeared to dislike each other intensely, because every time Lorenz and his dog went past the house the other terrier would rush out barking furiously, and then the two dogs would run the length of the picket fence, snarling, choking and spluttering at each other in desperate animosity.

One day the neighbor removed a section of the fence to repair it (not just because of the teethmarks!). The two animals went through their attack procedures all along the fence, until they came to the gap. There they came to a dead stop, noses inches apart, and stared nonplussed in silence at each other. Then, to Lorenz's amazement, they ran back to where the fence was intact and began again their barking and snarling routine. Old habits are hard to break, even nasty ones!

Trust

The primary change problem is one of lack of trust. A major reason for not trusting is because it means making yourself vulnerable, taking a chance with someone else, letting go the rock. This is something that business people in the West find very hard to do, particularly because of their organizational experiences. People have been treated as a means to someone else's ends, have been forced into artificially adversarial situations (often called "competitive"), and have had their creative potential ignored, or even worse, spurned. No wonder they generally employ a minimum-risk, keep your head down, strategy. Not everyone can be an organizational champion!

So, first of all top management need to let go their rock and take the human responsibility of running an organization with *people* in it very seriously. Secondly their management need to follow suit, and need to start "playing Reds," instead of playing management games. This absolutely must be done if the West is to develop the internal and external relationships which will allow us to compete more effectively in a rapidly shrinking world market.

The Buyer's Image

The first external barrier to overcome is that caused by the buyer and the buying department's image. The best way to start any change process it to take an honest look at the organization by looking at some examples of its behavior, and the reactions to it. So here are some images to reflect on.

The way the buyer is generally perceived today constitutes

one of the biggest barriers to gaining supplier cooperation. For example, Gavin Kennedy (1984), writing out of his experience as an international negotiation consultant, states "ask anybody who has been out in the real world about his [or her] atrocity stories of how buyers behave, and he or she is bound to include one of the following" and he goes on to list 16 horror stories, of which we will repeat five.

1   You will be kept waiting outside his office . . .
2   Other times, he meets you in the foyer of the waiting room with other people milling about and proceeds to conduct a conversation.
3   He gets your name and that of your company repeatedly wrong.
4   He looks bored—painfully bored—and stares as if he is not listening.
5   He will make discouraging remarks about you . . . he'll do the same about your product, your company . . . your track record and your chances.

In our own experience we know of a buyer in a food distribution chain in Great Britain who, when negotiating, turns his back on the seller and looks out of the window during the conversation, most often not even deigning to reply. If he is given product literature he drops it in the waste bin without even looking at it and is generally obnoxious. One of his major suppliers has seriously considered whether their purchases— which are big—are worth the effort required to maintain the relationship, just as Jerry, the entrepreneur, did in Chapter 4.

David Ogilvy of Ogilvy & Mather writes admiringly of Raymond Rubicam, head of Young & Rubicam, on this very point, when he describes the letter Rubicam wrote when he resigned the enormous American Tobacco account—a classic:

> Young & Rubicam and American Tobacco were both successful companies for some time before our association began. I trust both will continue to be successful companies after our association ceases, *which it is doing as of now.*

> (Ogilvy, 1983)

The reason for this letter? He disliked the bullying manner of the head of American Tobacco, George Washington Hill, which he felt was damaging the morale of his agency staff. But there is also another lesson from Rubicam, this time a positive one for suppliers. General Foods was Rubicam's biggest client and one day Rubicam told them that their account was too big for only one agency, and that a second and third should be hired. Subsequently, General Foods came to trust every recommendation Rubicam made to them.

Roger Pauli, chief executive of Stuart Crystal, the top-class lead-crystal producer in Britain, was prepared to sever his supplier relationship with Marks & Spencer in 1986 because their buyers could not handle his egalitarian style. Now that was a hard decision for Roger to make because Marks & Spencer is a fine company and is considered a real catch for any vendor; especially one as small as Stuart Crystal. However, they were not always as caring with their suppliers as they liked to think, and certainly at the interpersonal-behavior level there have been many complaints from suppliers which are typical of complaints about a paternalistic organization that is never quite as benevolent as it thinks it is. And it is salutary that even the hard-headed Gavin Kennedy actually states: "It is better not to deal at all than to negotiate under the duress of the buyer's intimidation" (1981).

Austin Rover (formerly British Leyland) also have a problem in that their smaller suppliers are still cynical about the way they are paid, i.e. late and uneven—which is critical for a small business. So, once again, the larger buyer needs to look to its *practices* if it really wants to get into a preferred-supplier relationship, and not just rely on public policy statements. The day we hear of the small suppliers commending Austin Rover on its payments policies, is the day we will believe that there has been a real shift in its attitude and that it genuinely has a new policy.

Yet against all of these negative experiences the United Kingdom Central Electricity Generating Board head of contracts, at the Institute of Purchasing and Supply Conference in January 1985, still called for suppliers to support buyers and "sell British." It was that kind of comment that caused a sales chief at the same conference to say that all he heard at the conference was a desire to optimize a buyer's profit(!), intimating that there was no reciprocal benefit for the suppliers. So, on the one hand, suppliers see buyers spending a lot of their time putting the suppliers down and, on the other hand, asking that the suppliers pay more attention to the buying organization's needs! No wonder suppliers are reluctant to "let go their rock."

The Supplier's Image

However, suppliers are not blameless. Buyers have been frustrated by slow responses to initial enquiries, badly worked-out proposals and at times dismissive replies to genuine requests for quotations. It is this lack of reaction which infuriates so many buyers. Here is a quote from a letter the purchasing officer of a manufacturer wrote in response to an article John Carlisle wrote criticizing purchasing companies for their lack of a relationships policy towards suppliers.

> I should like to refer to your editorial in the April edition of *Purchasing/Supplier Relationships*, and while endorsing John Carlisle's philosophy wholeheartedly, I feel that I must stress the old adage that "it takes two to tango".
>
> Whilst agreeing that company management need to take the initiative I feel we need to examine in which direction that initiative has to be channelled and, what is more important, the attitude of suppliers, and in particular UK suppliers which John Carlisle states that too many UK companies are all too willing to drop, need re-examining. . . .
>
> Now to suppliers—I am constantly amazed at the total lack of response of certain suppliers to various routine points that may arise. How many times, for example, have buyers to ring suppliers for quotations in reply to enquiries that may have been with them for a number of weeks. How many times are we fobbed off with false delivery promises, or lack of response to specification or technical answers. How many times do we ring up suppliers for a component or material we may be urgently awaiting for a breakdown, only to be told delivery will be 7/10 days, but he has an equivalent on the shelf which he does not offer to us, unless we ask the question.
>
> This I must regretfully say in my opinion is more apparent in UK suppliers than in overseas, and in certain instances we are forced to do what John Carlisle condemns us for, and drop that supplier and source overseas, usually with far better results and reliability. I often wonder if UK companies have in general, learned anything from the recession of the past few years.

Truly a cry from the heart!

Quality

Buyers have also been let down by supplying organizations on quality, delivery and service. British Leyland once had to return

22,040 components to different suppliers in just one month—overwhelmingly on grounds of quality. Suppliers have, at times, been guilty of being too greedy when it has been a seller's market, too anxious to get the business in a buyer's market through short-term price-cutting, and too reluctant to invest in new technology (very often because of their perception of the buyer's reluctance to help them achieve the payoff from that investment).

Initiative

Even in 1987 in Britain few suppliers were taking advantage of West Germany's adverse exchange rate to replace their components in the British car manufacturing market. And this is despite the additional fact that British labor costs were about $9 per hour compared with West Germany's $19. Bill Hayden, Ford of Europe's production director commented wryly to the effect that if the UK industry cannot compete when it is only paying half the German wage, there really was not much hope for them.

Returning to Austin Rover, to put the other side of the story, between 1982 and 1987 it reduced its supply base from 1200 to 700 companies, and forged long-term agreements with the remainder. However, there is still a lack of real investment by the suppliers in modern equipment and new technology and, so far as we can see, export manufacturing. So, not only are trust and efficiency major problems; but also, it seems, entrepreneurial risk-taking.

Finally, a supplier success story. The best-rated supplier we have come across is Ford (UK) Tractor Division. Their latest supply policies, including credit control and their attention to customer needs have really been extolled—unfortunately at the expense of GKN and Perkins—in the eyes of the smaller manufacturer. And all because senior management really are doing things more openly and really are becoming more visible in the marketplace and are seen to be standing behind their policies. This change is led by their vice-president of international sales, who has not barricaded himself in the USA; but who is making real human contact with the buyers and *listening* to them all over the world. Typical of these successful policies are:

1 A highly flexible, very cooperative technical department.
2 Helpful and flexible credit control department, who were described as particularly helpful when there was something of a crisis for one of their South Midlands buyers.
3 "From office boy to Managing Director they make us feel really like a customer." This was from the same buyer. They mentioned in particular the *Power Talk* magazine, which was topical and informative, as being part of that extra quality of service.

A final comment was: "GKN pushed us into the arms of Ford, and it would take wild horses to drag us away." Praise indeed!

These buyers, even the smallest, feel their needs are being met by Ford Tractor and that they are being treated properly, so they are going out more confidently into the marketplace to grow the business. This surely is what effective relationships are all about, and we believe that it is no coincidence that Ford also operates a successful preferred-supplier policy. Quality and customer orientation permeate an organization when management lead it properly, and a good supplier experience translates effortlessly into a satisfied customer.

POWER AND RESPONSIBILITY

Given these points which largely criticize buyer and supplier alike why is the onus for initiating change on the buying organization? To repeat, *because right now it is the buying organization which holds the power*. It is the buying organizaton which is in the position to really influence the relationship in a profound way by acknowledging the rights that the supplier has at individual, group and organizational level, and thereby encouraging the supplier and the buyer to take responsibility in the exercise of those rights. This is the enactment of interdependence and the discharge of moral obligation which Drucker urges again and again.

We now want to show how the buying organization can take initial responsibility for turning the supplier–buyer relationship into a healthy, long-term association, where rights are given and responsibilities taken equally, as each lets go their respective rocks and releases the creative potential which can enrich both their organizations.

Influencing Organizations

First of all, let us understand a basic law of influencing. The social world is composed of five levels of collectivities: individuals, groups, organizations, communities and societies. The law of influencing says that a collectivity can only successfully influence the next level above it. This means that individuals are not able to directly influence an organization—no matter where they are in the firm, top or bottom. Neither can a group directly influence a community; it needs an organization.

So, if a manager wishes to help his or her negotiators to influence their own, or the other, organization, they first need to set up an effective working group out of which that negotiator can work.

The first practical step is to set up a process which will lead to effective groups evolving within each organization, and between the buyer and seller, to allow the new purchasing policy to operate the way it was intended to. In the case of the preferred supplier a good route is to create an effective system whereby you can:

1 Select those criteria which will give definition to "preferred supplier." For example, Chrysler have a Pentastar Award which is given annually to their preferred suppliers on the basis of:

   (a) Quality (40% of total rating), meeting the new requirements for continually reducing the in-process variability.
   (b) Technology (20%), which includes not only being up-to-date, but also being willing to share research capabilities, to assist in design, and to help solve problems.

(c) Delivery (20%), which mainly revolves around being on time and flexible.

(d) Price competitiveness (20%), this is related to competitive pricing quotes, cost-saving policies, and adherence to Chrysler's standard payment terms.

Just recently, Chrysler have come up with another criterion: timely sample submissions and approvals for pilot and launch programs. This is in line with Western manufacturing concerns with matching Japanese rapid development cycles, which a US expert in product cycles in the automobile industry, Vladimir Pucik, has described as the "next battlefield" (*Wall Street Journal*, February 23, 1988). Honeywell, Allen-Bradley, Dana Corporation and the other more-aware manufacturers are looking at human technology, i.e. effective groups, as being as much their answer to the challenge as is hard technology.

2 Identify your best suppliers on a commodity basis—critical to this is competitive benchmarking.

3 Find out how they perceive you. This is the reality you will need to work with, then find out how they would *like* to see you. (Refer back to Chapter 6.)

4 Begin taking steps to really work together, using the final consumer's needs as your focus. Commit to a policy of cooperation by finding out what the suppliers' needs are, and by coming to an agreement as to what you can meet and how you intend meeting them. The Motorola survey results in Chapter 7 give an indication of these needs.

All this means beginning to give away some of your power, because you will never persuade anyone to "let go of their rock" while you are seen to be clinging on to yours! It turns out that this is an ideal assignment for the mandate team. If you are striving for an associative relationship with only the "preferred" suppliers of the more important commodities, it makes sense to use in that process only the people who know those commodities best. In a sense you will be creating something of a commodity-focused support group for the purpose of assuring that: (a) directives from above affecting this commodity are correctly understood and interpreted to others, (b) the needs of all members of the mandate team (planners and implementers) are taken into account, (c) the company utilizes the best available people for the procurement of this commodity, (d) all obligations of the firm incurred in this special relationship are discharged.

What better, then, than to assign this same team to the task of helping the buyer establish the associative relationship with the selected suppliers? And, once established, they become exactly the right group to monitor, support and maintain the relationship.

In a very real sense, what we have here is a "relationship quality circle" composed of the parties most concerned, and positioned to implement their own collective wisdom. They will need to possess or develop the skills to work with all of the disciplines affected by that commodity at different points in time, and to cultivate the many relationships needed to implement their ideas fully. They will be the policy-making board of directors for their micro-enterprise, with immediate access to their internal customer(s) and their internal or external supplier(s). As in conventional quality circles, the job-enrichment and self-fulfillment opportunities are considerable. And best of all, with the important constituencies all represented (including sales where appropriate) it should be possible to expect the mandate team to make their many decisions consistently in harmony with the consumer's best interests. In firms with major bought-in content, this focusing of the key decisions in the key commodities with the key suppliers should provide a powerful overall boost towards improving the likelihood of that important sale by meeting the consumer's needs better than the competitors can. And the mandate team can be held accountable for seeing that all decisions are made in the manner that senior management would make them. This is possible because they will be in fairly close contact with senior management in their role of interpreting directives, and can seek guidance whenever it is deemed necessary. It is advisable, however, that the mandate teams be identified and designed by the purchasing function to provide a balance among the functions. The mandate team should choose its own chairperson, and this should probably not be the purchasing member who may better serve as facilitator, scribe and secretary to keep the record of assignments, decisions and progress reports.

Setting Up the Relationship

The process for initiating this effort would best begin with an initial four-way assessment of perceptions of each other and of themselves by both supplier and supplied (see Table 8.1):

1   Key suppliers should identify those things the buying organization is doing which help or hinder development of this associative relationship.
2   Key suppliers should identify those things which they believe they are doing which help or hinder the development of this associative relationship.
3   The mandate team should identify those things the key suppliers are doing which help or hinder the development of the associative relationship.
4   The mandate teams should identify those things which they believe the buying organization is doing which help or hinder the development of the associative relationship.

Table 8.1   *Four-way perception assessment*

Their perception of our actions 1	Their perception of their actions 2
3 Our perception of their actions	4 Our perception of our actions

(See Appendix III for survey findings at a major automobile industry/electronics supplier conference in Detroit, October 1988.)

The list of these perceptions could form the agenda to be addressed by an early meeting between mandate teams and their key suppliers, particularly where the results indicate there may be significant differences in perception. There have been a number of supplier councils formed in the USA in the past few years. Some of them have been very creative in bringing about better communication between supplier and supplied, and good progress in resolving specific issues or launching specific quality or productivity programs. None, to our knowledge, has *started* with this insightful kind of four-way perception assessment: which is unfortunate in view of our finding that it is perceptions which really determine success or failure in the development of this relationship. So, quite often they have had to backtrack and then start testing perceptions because there have been some communications failures.

Initiating Trust

With the four-way analysis in hand, the mandate teams are once again precisely the right combination of specialized talent, experience and line authority to determine which of the relationship problems should be given priority treatment. They are best suited to know, or to determine, the likely return on any investment necessary to deal with a problem once identified, and they are therefore best suited to marshal the talent or resources and argue for necessary funds to deal with it. The key suppliers will be watching intently for this application of resources in view of the high level of skepticism mentioned earlier. Far too many well-intentioned programs have raised the supplier's hopes only to dash them on the rocks of implementation failure caused by a low level of trust and/or support. This can become a self-fulfilling prophecy leading to a downward spiral in the relationship. We can expect the mandate team, however, not to be too optimistic in their selection of projects as they will also be held responsible for their implementation.

Maintaining Trust

The mandate team is also the best-equipped and motivated body to provide or to monitor the provision of:

- Follow-up on agreed action steps by both customer and supplier activities to ensure that the relationship works.

- Support to the purchasing function in the negotiation of technical matters and the provision of supplier assistance as and when required to resolve problems which threaten the relationship.
- A sounding board for the purchasing function in its role as manager of the relationship.

Only after the mandate team has demonstrated its commitment to the relationship is it fully prepared to address the positive side of the opportunities here. This is again because the natural skepticism of suppliers, born out of experience, can only be laid to rest by some visible action on at least a few of the already existing problems. Once that demonstration of both intent and ability to make progress has occurred, there is a marvelous opportunity for both parties to brainstorm the positive questions, as in the Motorola example mentioned earlier. Again, Fisher and Ury have addressed this possibility and then listed the classic steps for a freewheeling creative session:

1 Separate the act of inventing options from the act of judging them.
2 Broaden the options on the table, rather than looking for a single idea. [Alex Osborn, father of brainstorming, called this "piggy-backing."]
3 Search for mutual gains (win–win!).
4 Invent ways of making their decisions easy.

MANAGEMENT PARTICIPATION

Having made the case for the management of the buying organization to free up the vendors to give their best attention to the customer's requirements, we now need to make a similar case for management to really face up to their workforce, including purchasing professionals, in order to help them to do the best possible job of working with the preferred supplier arrangement.

It seems that managers, caught as they are between the ideas of the top and the practices of the bottom, are very often the most reactionary and cautious members of an organization. When quality initiatives have foundered it has been because, more often than not, managers either have not kicked hard enough upwards or facilitated hard enough downwards. It is not surprising, in a sense, as we have seen some fine managers reduced to automatons as they have been forced to carry out unrealistic programs emanating from "theories" at the top. So it is no wonder they are as skeptical as most when it comes to more ideas for change.

However, what the quality movement above all else has demonstrated is that if management does let go and allows their subordinates to really participate in the work then there is a huge payoff. But this is all too infrequent, as far too often structured or technological devices are superimposed as a substitute for appropriate management involvement in setting up the right systems and motivation. This is a knee-jerk reaction which has to be changed.

Intellectual Capital

Ramchandran Jaikumar (1986), of the Harvard Business School, said: "the new role of management in manufacturing is to create and nurture the project teams whose intellectual capabilities produce competitive advantage. What gets managed is intellectual capital, not equipment." He went on to say: "I am convinced that the heart of this new manufacturing landscape is the management of manufacturing projects: selecting them, creating teams to work on them, and *managing workers' intellectual development.*"

The same point is made about the service industry by Townsend and Gebhardt (1986), when stressing the importance of quality teams in the fantastic productivity improvements in the Paul Revere Insurance Companies. They described them as a blend of "quality circles, supportive schemes, participative management and Yankee ingenuity." They then went on to quote from an American Productivity Center report:

> The basic idea that Deming had is this: If management is to be responsible for improving something as complicated as modern assembly of machines and people (whether in the factory, the hospital, the office or anywhere), managers must have a way of

learning (1) which parts of the problems are due to the workers and (2) which parts are due to the system.

We talk far took often of worker participation when, in fact, we should be encouraging *manager participation*. Participating by really taking an interest in those performances of the suppliers that facilitate good work, and those that block good work; participation by really getting involved in the people problems; participation by taking ownership of the final product and its fitness for purpose; participation by actively facilitating teamwork and getting down to understanding how groups really work together. This intelligent participation forms the essence of the micro-strategy.

A great deal has been written about team procedures, structures and behaviors in order to help managers develop effective teams. However, what has been missing is that sense of development, that time dimension, which relates to the life of a group. Groups, like all living things, have an organic nature, which means that once they are put together they go through a growth and maturation process over time. So whatever training is applied must take cognizance of where that particular group is in terms of its own development. Managers in particular need to understand this, not least because if they are not careful, the group will outgrow them. Hence this next section explaining how groups grow and develop, which is specifically for managers of teams—especially mandate teams.

MANDATE TEAMS AND GROUP DEVELOPMENT

We strongly believe that the mandate team is the answer to achieving a creative, buyer–seller relationship which generates competitive advantage for both parties, and there is a rapidly growing body of evidence to support this conviction. There is also ample history to indicate that such multidiscipline groups, once formed, are very tender organisms at first, and require very special care and feeding to survive their infancy. They require the right conditions and a healthy level of encouragement as they learn to crawl, if they are to accept the inevitable bruises from falling and yet persist until they learn how best to walk and ultimately to run. There is a pattern of hazards and crisis points through which they must develop if they are to mature, just as there is a series of hazards and crisis points through which adolescents must pass as they mature and develop. This group development is not smooth; rather it is "discontinuous," meaning the growth is characterized by phases in exactly the same fashion as the organization phases in Chapter 5.

Each phase is separated by a crisis (which in Greek means "decision-point," when things come apart at the seams and relationships can become quite strained). This is what is known as a *threshold*, and people feel quite weary at this point and often prefer to retreat to the more familiar group behavior. However, those groups which persist will go on to successively more effective stages of development, gaining increasingly greater capacities for understanding situations, and helping the negotiator in making really well-judged decisions.

Only a mature, healthy group permits a mature, healthy negotiation.

To repeat, an effective mandate team does not just happen—it develops over time and with no little struggle. So, if a group is to arrive at the point where it is of real assistance to the negotiator in planning then it has to grow and develop. This means:

1 Its history will not be smooth: there will have been ups and downs, but the trend will be "better."
2 There will have been distinct "crisis" periods where it will have had really to take stock of its function and ways of working. These are usually recognized by tensions arising, most often caused by a feeling of being "stuck."
3 It will be almost a different group after each crisis, capable of addressing different issues in new ways. This sometimes means it will outgrow some of its members.

We will present a framework which illustrates these changes. But first, you are invited to determine the phase of development one of your own groups has reached. Think of a group in which you participate. If possible, it should be a group whose support would help you make, and carry out, decisions at work, and which includes members who need to be satisfied by your behavior or the results of your behavior. Picture your last few meetings with that group, then answer the following questions as they would apply to just those last few meetings.

PHASES QUESTIONNAIRE

In your last few meetings:

	Yes	Perhaps	No
(1) Did you feel totally at ease?	___	___	___
Was the group acting as a group?	___	___	___
Did it seem to understand the task fully?	___	___	___

	Yes	Perhaps	No
(2) Was there a bit of in-fighting?	___	___	___
Did people wander away from the aims occasionally?	___	___	___
Were more honest opinions expressed?	___	___	___

	Yes	Perhaps	No
(3) Did you feel it was more under control?	___	___	___
Did you feel frustrated that some important issues were not discussed enough?	___	___	___
Were there some quite negative personal feelings expressed?	___	___	___

	Yes	Perhaps	No
(4) Was it a dull meeting?	___	___	___
Did you see some really interesting facets of people emerging?	___	___	___
Did the meeting really "take-off" at times, with people enjoying it?	___	___	___

	Yes	Perhaps	No
(5) Was time handled early and clearly?	___	___	___
Were people up-tight?	___	___	___
Was nearly everyone committed to the objectives and solutions?	___	___	___

	Yes	Perhaps	No
(6) Was it fun?	___	___	___
Were the solutions quite original?	___	___	___
Were people really interested in each other?	___	___	___

	Yes	Perhaps	No
If the ground had been disbanded:			
(7) Are you pleased at your accomplishment?	___	___	___
Are you sad it is over?	___	___	___
Do you respect your ex-colleagues?	___	___	___

Now read the "Phases of Group Development" section which follows and then score your answers according to the answer sheet at the end to see if you can determine approximately in what phase your group was functioning during those meetings. If you are able to conclude that it was operating at a given level, you should find your feelings about the capacity of the group confirmed. You may also find the capacity associated with the next higher level to be of interest as that is the improvement in the quality of group behavior to which you can most immediately aspire.

PHASES OF GROUP DEVELOPMENT

When a group of people meet for the first time, especially a multidisciplinary group, for the purpose of becoming a team, then it is really important to understand the problems they will need to go through if the group is to mature. This process has to be managed, just as everything else at work, so it first has to be understood.

Early on . . .

Although people are there for a common purpose, their individual intentions will differ. Some will be aware of these intentions, others will be less so. So already there are some disparities which will need to be dealt with. There will also be differing motivations which arise from a combination of each individuals' own:

- understanding of the objective,
- feelings towards it as understood,
- needs level; existence; relatedness and growth needs.

Contact

There will also be a mixture of ways of thinking, such as engineering as against purchasing; and different experiences of suppliers, standards and of the organization. These will give rise to differing reactions, not just to the issues, but also to the very fact of being in a working group.

So there is a good deal of uncertainty surrounding that first meeting. The only basis for certainty that people have is the visible presence of several other people in the room and, within themselves, the awareness of their own positions and past experience. Whether this experience will be of any use in this new situation is something they cannot yet tell.

If people are uncertain, they tend to look for a source of certainty. So first they look to the person responsible for the meeting, thinking that he or she must know more about what should happen than the others. The person with the formal authority will be regarded as the one that should bring struc-ture (certainty) to the group. The group then tends to become dependent on this person; not wanting to take responsibility, and asking what they should do. This initial stage is *depend-ency*, and if the manager responds to this as a "parent," and takes responsibility for the group, then this in itself will prevent the group from taking responsibility for itself and maturing.

However, if the group is to become responsible for its own development, and is to face up to its own crises, then there is quite a lot the manager can do to prepare them. For example, talk with each person before they meet and explain the purpose behind the group formation, the rationale and the task to be performed. Also explain the process and procedures. Repeat this at the first meeting, encourage questions and answer them; but also ask for opinions. Then, with or without appointing a leader, leave them to address the task.

If the members of the group feel somewhat more certain because of the elementary hygiene steps the manager has taken, they then progress through these first stages quite quickly. If, however, they are still not clear, they will do what we all do when we are uncertain and minimize personal risk by wearing professional "masks" all the time and looking for either simple solutions or someone to blame for not getting anywhere. This will lead to a dissatisfied, low-performing group and this will reflect in low-quality outputs and rela-tionships both inside and outside the organization.

Maneuvering

If the group is more or less forced to take responsibility for itself, one person in the group will probably take up the challenge and become the informal leader. But it is possible that others in the group also want this role, so something like a struggle for leadership can start. Others may withdraw for the time being and "sit on the fence" waiting for the winner to become visible. Supporters for each of the parties can be identified by the way they back proposals from the different parties. Their support is often emotionally loaded and may be given through value judgments. They will also tend then to support each other so that group building starts within these subgroups, very often aligned with people's expertise and shared experience.

Adapted

The important thing in this continuous process of interaction is that the different personal viewpoints become visible to the members of the group. They start to *see each other's* viewpoints. At this time a first image of the common objective may also become visible. Members of the group may begin to see the sense of the *group objective*. They can begin to see the relationship between their own objectives and the common group objective. The members of the group may even start to change their own perception of the group objective in this orientation process. Then something like a group image of the objective may arise. This gives a vague, subconscious feeling of belonging, based on a common awareness of having, for the first time, met on an intellectual level. So they begin to work together more appropriately, at least formally.

Later on . . .

There is an important shift after these three phases as the individuals really begin to meet each other, and themselves, without their masks, to get down to a real understanding of the task. People challenge each other more, and real exploration of the issues starts to take place. Patrick Townsend in writing about setting up the Quality Steering Committee in the Paul Revere organization (Townsend and Gebhardt, 1986) says: "At first glance—and at the time—it appeared that the Quality Steering Committee wasted its first several meetings," and that "subsequent discussions in the Quality Steering Committee meetings were heated at times." People had really begun to encounter each other!

Encounter

By now, the members of the group are better known to each other and can start working together. They have a clearer idea of their objectives—which does not, however, mean they all agree with them. Individual habits, speech mannerisms and, moreover, strengths and weaknesses will become evident. Some of these marks of individuality can aid the group when used at the right time, but they can also prove to be an irritant as untimely intrusions. So the group is now becoming conscious of the quality of interactions, although not necessarily understanding the cause.

There are strengths and weaknesses in everyone; the former are not always recognized by others; the latter are not always recognized by ourselves. In every human being there is always a battle going on between being in favor of the group's objectives (selflessness) and having one's own agenda. There is also the tendency to see the less attractive qualities of the other person first; but very often those that are most irritating are those that are most prominent in oneself.

If a group of people now have to work very closely together, all these personal points can "get on one's nerves." When a group becomes conscious of this problem, alternative solutions are normally seen. Both have disadvantages, through being one-sided, and do not really aid group development.

1   *The emotional response.* Someone starts a quarrel or a row. The group tends to fall apart into subgroups. People may walk out, etc. In fact the group is regressing.
2   *The rational response.* Personal differences and problems are papered over by a procedure. ("Let's not get personal,

ladies and gentlemen, we must stick to our task.") A formal division of tasks may be used to formalize the procedure and avoid the personal encounter (which seems to be dangerous). A formal chairperson and/or scribe may be appointed; a formal agenda, time schedules, etc., may appear.

But these standard solutions to the group's problems can overrule personal wishes and desires and can thus stifle initiative and creativity. Neither really solves the problem of "growing up."

There is a third approach which allows the safety-valve to open up a bit, so that excess pressure may blow off and guide the remaining energy through the normal channels to keep the engine working. An important part of this is the courageous step of giving and taking personal feedback, because members of the group must really become conscious of their problem, know what to do about it, and also want to do something about it. In other words, the members of the group must act with inward consciousness and as mature human beings. Feedback is essential to this, as is the worthwhileness of the task.

Effective

As members begin both to give and to accept personal feedback, a second feeling of belonging, which has been gathering strength, can arise. This feeling is based on the fact that one begins to realize that every human being is different and that these differences are not only a problem but can also be a source of creativity for the group. People are willing to accept the other human being as different and try to make use of these different abilities to further the group objective. For individuals this means trying to hold back those personal traits that can hinder the group in reaching the objective. They may need to sacrifice part of their personal wishes so as really to understand what is needed.

To return to Patrick Townsend and his experiences with the

setting up of the Quality Steering Committee (1986), he went on to say that these early meetings, which were described as "messing about with quality," were crucial. They asked themselves, what quality really meant, "what does it mean to us?"—a crucial question—and this led to the birth of a distinctive vocabulary which was much more appropriate to what the organization needed. This approach—"messing around," using this vocabulary—was recommended for all new groups to adopt as they entered the quality process.

The same process was encountered by the Portable Instruments Division of Tektronix, as they launched their first "mandate" group after hearing Bob Parker explain the concept. They too had to mess around; but on sticking at it, they found that they were forced to look at, and share, and contrast, their own values about the work. Once this was done, the team really took off.

When John Carlisle met some of them in mid 1987, it was obvious that they were members of a successful team, i.e. relaxed, self-assured and competent; but also somewhat irritatingly so—typical attributes of an "in-group." They needed to be looking to enter the next phase; which is another big step.

Creative

Now a new level of cooperation can arise where every member of the group tries, as much as they can, consciously to:

- bring in their abilities, insofar as these help the group to reach considered judgments;

- hold back their prejudices, which would otherwise hinder the group process;

- observe and sense the interaction between the members of the group;

- use evaluations (objectively describing phenomena that occur) to make the group conscious of what is going on, at the interaction, content and procedural levels;

- learn from these evaluations and thus gain self-knowledge;
- become a fully responsible group member, thinking and behaving intelligently with a sense of the corporate and group objective.

This leads to some tremendous creative, and yet thoughtful, solutions and ideas as the synergy grows. The ability to engage in objective *reflection and evaluation* is one of the two outward signs of a mature group. (The other is the ease with which they take in newcomers to the group so that they are quickly and painlessly on board.)

An important feature of this process of evaluating is that people normally learn best when they are in charge of their own learning. It may be possible to guide a person toward some self-knowledge by the judicious use of questions, but rarely, if ever, will they learn from the many statements and value judgments of others, no matter how well intended. A key management role here is to hold confidential, informal debriefing sessions with individual members and to counsel where necessary.

In working together like this, a still stronger bond can arise. It is a feeling of belonging which goes beyond personal feelings. It is based on the fact that as a group member one realizes that the group not only needs different members to be as different as they are to enrich the possibilities of the group, but also that the individuals of the group all have their own personal struggles and their individual paths of development, which might be quite different from that of others. Experiencing this fact can give one a feeling of responsibility, for the group and for its members. The question may form "what should we (or I) do to help any of the other individuals in the group to overcome their problems and to develop themselves even further, so that they can become an even more valuable member of our group?"

This last feeling of belonging is still very rare in groups. It can be seen in groups which have had to work together over a long period of time. Very often these feelings arise after a group has gone through several crises and the members have come to the conclusion that only unity in differentiation, and mutual responsibility for each other as human beings, are real sources of strength in reaching a group objective. (There's an old black American proverb which runs: "Your only true friends are the ones you've cried with"!)

Moving on . . .

Really mature groups know when their task together is finished, and they address this crisis as openly as all the others. Every human process has a birth, a life and a death phase, and groups are no exception.

Dissolving

A group that has completed its mission is often reluctant to admit it. They will often invent reasons for staying together, stretching out the task, using more investigations, and in general delaying the end. But finally someone raises the issue, and the really good team addresses its closure as it would any other group issue. They decide on how they should dissolve, what tidying up needs to be done, and how best to communicate it.

They also evaluate honestly and clearly what they have achieved together and celebrate this in a way that is meaningful for them. And if this is all carried out in a proper fashion they will, like the healthy fruit, become the seeds of many other successful group initiations in the organization.

Here again, the manager plays a vital role in allowing the due processes to occur; in acknowledging their understanding of what needs to be done, by being openly grateful not just for their achievement, but also for their struggles together in, and for, the organization. And the reward for the managers is that, through the risks taken for real development, they grow them-

PHASES QUESTIONNAIRE—ANSWERS

Typical of:

Answers (1) 3 Nos   = phase 1—Contact
        (2) 3 Yesses   = phase 2—Maneuvering
        (3) 3 Yesses   = phase 3—Adapted
        (4) No, Yes, Yes = phase 4—Encounter
        (5) Yes, No, Yes = phase 5—Effective
        (6) 3 Yesses   = phase 6—Creative
        (7) 3 Yesses   = phase 7—Dissolving

The questionnaire is not meant to be precise, and if your answers lead you to two, or perhaps more, of the phases, then you are probably at a threshold, which means you should check the model to see what the next step is.

Capacities
It takes a long time to get to phase 7—sometimes years. But most groups can at least get to the Adapted phase by the end of two days working together. The Encounter phase, which is a sort of threshold on its own, is often very difficult and could need a facilitator to help work through some of the deeper personal issues which frustrate people, but which they will not confront. The more you work these through, the greater capacities you will have.

Phase	*Capacity*
Contact:	Very simple task planning.
Maneuvering:	More advanced planning, with clearer goals.
Adapted:	Good task planning; but often quite low commitment.
Encounter:	Good judgment exercised, real decisions, higher commitment.
Effective:	Thorough planning, satisfying process and quality decisions.
Creative:	Excellent judgment, many insights, innovative solutions—but often also very questioning of organizational competence.
Dissolving:	Real human approaches, deeper respect for people, great capacity for understanding groups, which is taken to other groups members join.

selves, not into more senior managers, but into leaders, which is what we so desperately need in industry today.

Having assessed your own group capabilities, it is now useful to study the characteristics of each phase in more detail and to look at the thresholds which must be crossed at each crisis point if the group is to achieve the capacities of the next phase.

BOILING FROG SYNDROME

It is a physiological fact that the frog has a great ability to adapt to the ever-changing temperature of its watery environment. It is also a fact that it does not like extreme temperatures, and if dropped into a pan of boiling water, will jump out immediately, little the worse for the experience.

It is said to be equally true that a frog placed in a pan of cold water which is slowly brought to a boil will make heroic efforts to adjust to the bad situation, but will die when the water boils without having thought to jump out.

This presents the opportunity to guide any group you wish across the threshold when you recognize that they are a bit "stuck." It also gives you a much better alternative than to suffer from the "boiling frog" syndrome we so often observe.

The ability to recognize a particular crisis point would have been very helpful to the frog. The indication at each threshold should be useful when considering how best to move a group to its next phase of development. The goal should usually be to help any multidiscipline group develop to its creative phase, where the differences between its members—which will always be there—*contribute* to their creativity instead of impeding it.

The problem most frequently encountered in launching mandate teams is half-solved by recognizing that each and every one of them will bump into the handicaps implied in each of the above phases. It follows that a particular mandate team is far more likely to pass over each threshold safely if its members address that crisis point consciously, and with some understanding of its nature. It was only when the Tektronix commodity teams, mentioned earlier, struggled through the "pain and agony" of reaching full agreement on the *criteria* for selecting their preferred suppliers that they became truly candid with each other and moved on past the Adapted phase where so many groups get stuck in what can prove to be near-boiling water.

Table 8.2   *Summary of the phases of group development*

	Phase of development	Typical comments
Contact	Weighing each other up Pretty cautious with each other; but open about their relation to the task Talking out of their professional "masks", not personally No deep questions; shallow approach People feel uneasy; but usually a bit of nervous laughter	"Hey, what's this all about?" "I don't really know why I am here" "This meeting does not seem to be getting anywhere"
	Threshold crossing Start to bring in basic procedures for handling the task, including role allocation	
Maneuvering	Some attempt to choose a chairperson Subgroups begin to form Demands for clarity of objectives Some struggle with the leader Some opt out People start exploring ideas with each other and challenge these Gets a bit more personal	"Look, that won't work" "I agree with Ted" "I think we should aim for . . ." "Well, that may be how you see it; but what's really happening . . ."
	Threshold crossing Start to share and contrast aims and objectives; personal aims versus group aims	
Adapted	Task aims are clearer Roles accepted Begin to work together more appropriately, in a formal sort of way Procedurally competent Deeper questions of what and how Ways of handling the time are discussed But also frustrations may be expressed	"Just stick to the plan" "Will someone take the minutes" "There's no time to worry about personal issues" "You're wasting our time again" "I *told* you it would not work"

Table 8.2 *Continued*

Phase of development		Typical comments
	Feelings may rise to the surface and are expressed personally	
	Threshold crossing Personal values begin to be expressed. Feelings about each are made public and some arguments ensue. Everyone begins to evaluate the task and the process in a more imaginative way	
Encounter/ meeting	Decide to tackle personal issues consciously Begin to look at how they work together Challenge how they see others working—or not working Feelings not bottled up; but expressed as they occur People valued for their individual contributions— not for their roles Takes time to address relationship issues	"I would like you not to stick to the rules for once" "Would someone help me, I'm really stuck" "Hey, you have just interrupted me again" "What do you know, he's human!" (Some laughter as well as the challenges).
	Threshold crossing Start to assemble real options in terms of what individuals really want to happen, i.e. personal values expressed. Simple solutions are rejected as longer term is brought in, and more imaginative approaches arise	
Effective	Flexibility in roles and procedures Options more carefully weighed Clear problem-analysis Implications, good and bad, are looked at carefully Solutions looked at over time, and attention paid to implementation Priorities clearly established People are relaxed and busy	"We need to decide where best to spend our time" "Can we just look again at why we're doing this?" "Why don't some of us work on this, while you work on that?"

Table 8.2   *Continued*

Phase of development		Typical comments
	Threshold crossing Time is under control and is not allowed to exert the same pressure. Always time for review. The group's values are assessed in relation to the task. Quality becomes an issue. Individuals want to try things for their *own* development, not just procedurally or task oriented	
Creative	People really enjoy problem-solving together, with a real interest in each other They use their differences creatively Handling of relationships at the same time as the tasks Praise is given and received Help offered and received A sense of belonging to the group emerges, very often expressed by looking for another task to do together	"Why don't we let Dave get on with that, while you and I put this one together?" "That's brilliant" "Hey, we need some thinking here, will you two join us" "It seems a pity to have to stop"
	Threshold crossing Relationships and outcomes feedback are objectively received. Quality in both becomes a high priority. Tasks and meetings are tidied up, past and future are looked at clearly (and courageously). Some desire to hold on to the "good old times"	
Dissolving	Consciousness of group no longer having a purpose Decisions on how to end it Revisiting what has been learned A sense of loss; but also of fulfillment, and gratitude	"We need to ask if we are still needed" "Shall we finish this and then have a farewell drink?" "I am really going to miss you guys. We did a good job. Thanks"

Finally, to return to the theme of interdependence and cooperation as a competitive strategy, how does management empower mandate teams to interact effectively internally and externally in order to grow the associative relationship? The answer is that mandate teams must be allowed three specific freedoms by the organization:

1 *Freedom of thought.* The team needs access, and the right, to use all available information, so that their members can build an accurate picture of the situation. All ideas are then welcome—no matter what the discipline is of the person who offers it.

2 *Freedom of feeling.* Everyone in the team should have the right to express their feelings about issues, so that balanced "head and heart" decisions are formed out of their collective judgments. These judgments should carry authority throughout the organization, and senior managers, in particular, should pay attention to them.

3 *Freedom of action.* Once a specific issue is agreed by the team, then the person who takes responsibility for making and implementing the final decision must be given full authority so to do. This is the essence of mandating, and is the ultimate goal of the mandate team. There is a popular fallacy that effective teams make the best decisions. This is not the case. Effective teams help individual members arrive at sound, informed (balanced) judgments, out of which the best qualified member makes the best decision—with confidence.

SUMMARY

We have taken you through a mega-strategy based on the vision of preferred-supplier arrangements, and have presented the idea of a macro-strategy oriented around the establishment of mandate teams to arrive most efficiently at the associative relationship which makes the most of preferred suppliers. Both of these strategies are mediated by the phase of development the organization is in, and by the effectiveness of the conditions which management creates around them. Finally, the micro-strategy outlined in this chapter leads to effective, developing, groups that grow good negotiators, who, in turn, foster healthy, creative relationships.

And that brings us full circle from idea to reality, from cooperation as a possibility, to cooperation as a profitable fact.

SELECTED READINGS

Kennedy, G., Benson, J. and McMillan, J. *Managing Negotiations.* Business Books, London (1980).

Kennedy, G. *Everything is Negotiable.* Arrow Books, London (1984).

Jaikumar, R. "Postindustrial Manufacturing," *Harvard Business Review.* November–December, pp. 69–76 (1986).

Ogilvy, D. *Ogilvy on Advertising.* Pan Books, London (1983).

Pascale, R. and Athos, A. *The Art of Japanese Management.* Penguin, Harmondsworth (1982).

Purchasing, "Medal of Professional Excellence Award," to Xerox, June 27 (1985).

Townsend, P. and Gebhardt, J. *Commit to Quality.* John Wiley, Chichester (1986).

9
Conclusion

Our intention throughout this book has been to help develop a deeper understanding of the nature of interdependent relationships, especially those which develop between a customer firm and a key supplier. It is clearly the experience of a number of thoughtful companies that this relationship is a determining factor in their efforts to gain competitive advantage in the marketplace by causing key suppliers to favor them with their best ideas and efforts.

We have made what we believe is a powerful case for concluding that cooperation between customer and key supplier is a far better strategy for attracting this preferential treatment than the more traditional adversarial approach which may have produced regular short-term advantages—but only so long as all customer firms played by roughly those same rules. And Axelrod makes a powerful case that such cooperation grows only from anticipated reciprocal cooperation.

Since we started this book many fundamental changes in attitude have occurred in the West. The most important has obviously been that initiated by Gorbachev in the arms race. If ever a man understood the value of finding ways to live together by working on joint interests, he has. Remember his phrase "Great nations don't have friends, they have interests"? The other sea-change is the opening up of the European Community as a free market for its members in 1992. Even the

British public are becoming aware of the opportunities over the English Channel—which is a major step for a bunch of islanders! Negotiations about joint ventures are taking place everywhere, and collaboration is the message—if not the medium!

For John Carlisle, in particular, there is something happening in his own city of Sheffield (the US equivalent is Pittsburgh) which is uplifting and which could become a beacon to many. Sheffield is controlled by a left-wing Labour Council. It sees itself, by and large, as a city that is protective of the working class, and of the disadvantaged—by whatever definition—and it has attracted such epithets as the "loony left" from right-wing elements in the larger society. For many years Sheffield council has had an adversarial relationship with the local "capitalists," the business organizations. Partly as a consequence of this, and of an uncompromising stance by the government towards Sheffield, and other Labour-controlled cities, the city went into a steep decline during the recession of the 1980s. However, in the last 18 months the leader of the Council, Clive Betts, and prominent business people, such as Richard Field and Norman Adsetts (successive presidents of the Chamber of Commerce), have got together over the common ground of revitalizing Sheffield.

The decline has stopped, recovery is beginning, and the quality of life has a good chance of really changing for the better—if people can distinguish between enterprise and opportunism! Joint initiatives are springing up everywhere, of which the most noteworthy is that between the Local Education Authority and local business. It is innovative, purposeful, and has real vision. After all, the buyer–supplier relationship can never be more important than when the key customers are the children. This is a typical good piece of enterprise, and if the momentum for "Partnership in Enterprise" is sustained, and it has some real champions, then a great city will be reborn, and will become an inspiration to many other struggling manufacturing centers throughout the world. If it fails, it will be because local politicians and business people have not been sufficiently prepared to work on themselves and their relationships. A great opportunity will have been lost!!

So, as a microcosm of this societal wave of change, following, not leading, the business movement, corporations need to see themselves as part of a fraternity whose profits are an indication of how they have best met their consumers' needs. Thus they need to work out of what Hayes and Wheelwright (1984) call a "productive confederation." For the successful businesses this productivity is underpinned by good supplier relationships. However, those firms that refuse the opportunity to cooperate with their best suppliers may well find themselves out of business. World-class suppliers cannot, by definition, give preferential treatment to everyone. Those producers who are the first to establish the right relationships will have a built-in advantage over those who come later. They will have crossed what is the last remaining frontier for competitive advantage in the West, given that Total Quality is at last beginning to be taken seriously.

Nevertheless, in order to be realistic, we had to point out the pitfalls, inner and outer, that exist. We emphasized the two human obstacles to developing an associative relationship, i.e. our individual reluctance to take risks with people and, related to it, our difficulty in trusting others.

When we add to these obstacles those organizational forces working against a healthy buyer–seller relationship—in particular those constraints imposed by the rational/scientific organizations, in which most people are employed—then it seems almost miraculous that any two complex organizations can possibly work together. However, as the Sheffield example and some of the recent manufacturing successes show, a bit of real leadership and willpower for cooperation goes a long way. And once people realize that groups are their most powerful agents for change, especially lower down in the organization, they will find ways of doing what they have always known intuitively should be done, i.e. cooperate, not compete, to serve the final consumer best. This puts heart back into firms and people who are overstressed by complexity, and the ever-quickening pace of change in society today.

We have said that mandate teams are the key, and we say this because evidence is coming in from all over the industrialized world that the formal and informal groups set up for the purpose of continuous improvement, in whatever sphere, are the engines of real change in the organization.

These multidiscipline teams, under a variety of names, are appearing in more and more of the better firms and are proving particularly adept at managing the attitude and relationship questions which lie between upper managements' broad objectives and the specific tasks necessary to achieving them. In the process of interpreting those broad objectives downward, the mandate teams perform a vital service by feeding a large dose of reality back to upper management in a way which significantly improves the quality of the decision-process at the top.

We have pointed out that groups such as these emerging mandate teams tend to get stuck in certain phases of their development. But they also can be helped through the internal crises which then occur, and thus be made able to progress to the next level of capability. The passage through each threshold to the next phase of development can be greatly aided by explicitly addressing the constraints, and by facing up to the personal shortcomings and value differences between individuals which work against such transformation.

In the end, real competitiveness must start at the top, with good business strategies based on the realities of the business. Only upper management can provide the right internal conditions for creating and sustaining an effective buyer–supplier relationship which will turn on the flow of competitive advantage so often found to be waiting there. So, if any readers who, as top managers, think we have been a bit hard on you, then we are sorry; but we stand by our views. The world of work is crying out for inspiring leadership. A very recent survey discussed in the Institute of Directors' magazine, *Director* (1988), states that 70% of the executives interviewed in the survey saw the recent decline in industrial success as attributable to a dearth of leadership. The main areas highlighted were lack of vision and imagination, and remoteness. So, staying helpfully in touch when problems arise, as they inevitably will, even in associative relationships, is a major task for top managers. More important, they will need to find new ways and forms of helping their managers stay involved without them interfering either, because they will need the skills to help resolve each problem that occurs in such a way that strengthens, rather than weakens, this pivotal associative relationship. This is so that the climate can be created in which enlightened negotiations can take place in a way that recognizes the underlying needs of both parties, even when there is a possible conflict.

Relationship management, therefore, through the mandate

teams, and sustained by the right leadership, will carry the buyer–supplier relationship "beyond negotiation" to a higher level of consciousness of what can and needs to be done. This heightened awareness of what qualities people have to offer, and what quality of life they deserve, will lead to that outstanding quality of service which customers everywhere are coming to expect.

SELECTED REFERENCES

Crainer, S. "A Question of Leadership," *Director*, June, pp. 117–118 (1988).

Hayes, R. and Wheelwright, S. *Restoring our Competitive Edge— Competing through Manufacturing*. John Wiley, New York (1984).

Appendix I

Guidelines for selecting the mandate team (as given to participants on "Getting Preferential Treatment" training courses).

Definition: The members of a Mandate Team are those people whose presence is necessary and sufficient for a given negotiable objective to be implemented. In drawing up and implementing successful agreements they would be those to whom everyone in the firm (including the Chairman) would turn to ask, "What are your minimum needs which must be met if your function is to lend its full support to achieving this aim?"

The people who own and communicate those minimum needs (mandates) can usually be identified by looking at the major areas of activity.

Where the objective involves an idea, a product or a service, the list will often look something like this:

design	the person responsible for the creation, design or designability of the idea, product or service which lies at the heart of the objective being addressed
production	the person responsible for the production or producibility or procurement of that idea, product or service
cost	the person responsible for the cost or affordability of that idea, product or service
sales	the person responsible for the delivery, sale or saleability of that idea, product or service

and   ⎧ any others whose support is essential to reach-
          ⎪ ing your chosen objective and whose specific
          ⎨ minimum needs must be met in any chosen
          ⎪ course of action if you are to receive that
          ⎩ support

As an aid in identifying these Mandate Teams in your life, it is helpful to visualize productive work as largely a channel of events which transform some of Mother Earth's materials, space or time into a product or service for ultimate consumption.

This produces the following picture:

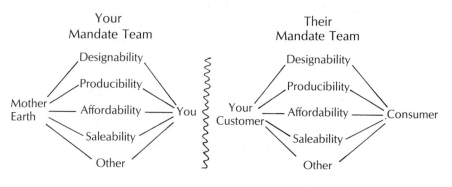

Appendix II

An extract from Ford Manufacturing Engineering and Purchasing's circular on their process to select preferred suppliers for simultaneous engineering projects, issued in 1988.

FACILITIES AND TOOLING
SIMULTANEOUS ENGINEERING PROCEDURE

- Manufacturing Engineering and Purchasing will identify major facility and tooling systems that will be presourced on new product programs.

- Two or three sources will be selected by Engineering and Purchasing for each of the preselected facility and tool requirements. The sources will be selected 43 to 50 months prior to vehicle Job 1 and will be requested to develop concept proposals with benchmark pricing. At a group line-up, the suppliers will be presented with preliminary quoting guidelines including early engineering released drawings or similar surrogate product design information for concept proposal development. Purchasing confirms arrangement by way of letter.

- In some cases, Engineering and Purchasing will agree that only one supplier possesses the required expertise and resources for the proposed development program, thereby negating the requirement for competitive proposals. This is most likely to occur when a supplier has successfully completed a simultaneous engineering project on a similar product.

- Ford reviews submitted proposals and selects one supplier with consideration extended to both process concept and benchmark cost. Purchasing will issue a letter of commitment to the supplier. The letter should precede program approval by at least 12 months (43 months prior to Job 1) to allow a minimum of 12 months of simultaneous engineering effort.

- The selected supplier joins the simultaneous engineering team consisting of Ford Product and Manufacturing Engineering. The team will develop the optimum process and provide the supplier with the opportunity to suggest product changes that improve the process while retaining product design, integrity, and quality.

- After 3 months of simultaneous engineering, the supplier, Engineering and Purchasing, will agree upon a target price using the benchmark proposal and accumulated simultaneous engineering experience. With target price approval, the supplier will continue simultaneous engineering effort to develop an optimum process and submit a firm price quotation to Purchasing for the process prior to program approval. If an acceptable target price cannot be negotiated, an alternate presource should be considered or we will submit the requirements to competitive bidding.

- Immediately after program approval, place a firm, final purchase order with the supplier for the preselected facility or tooling item.

Appendix III

DETROIT IMAGINOLOGY WORKSHOP OCTOBER 1988 RESPONSES TO THE QUERY:

"What does the Automobile/Electronics Industry *need* from the Electronics/Automobile Industry—which either is *not* now getting?"

EXECUTIVE SUMMARY*

Supplier   Customer

We need you to plan more closely with us

We need you to understand us better

We need greater commitment from you

We need better execution by you

Key: Electronics Industry comments in this category

Automobile Industry comments in this category

Consensus Conclusions

- Is the relationship between the Automobile and Electronics Industries good? **NO**
- Why is it not good? **LACK OF TRUST IN EACH OTHER**
- What is the prime cause of this lack of trust in each other?

A PATTERN OF FAILURE BY *BOTH* PARTIES FULLY AND FAITHFULLY TO DELIVER THAT WHICH HAS BEEN PROMISED

(Which has led to the Western Automobile Industry being overtaken by the Japanese!)

*Attached are the verbatim comments as developed by the participants plus the implications and conclusions drawn from them by the workshop facilitators.

Carlisle & Parker
22 October, 1988

RELATIONSHIP MANAGEMENT TECHNOLOGY
for
GLOBAL COMPETITIVE ADVANTAGE

On October 19, 20 and 21, 1988, Motorola presented the Imaginology Exhibit at Detroit's Cobo Hall immediately following the Dearborn Convergence Conference between the Automobile and Electronics Industries. As part of the Seminar Series on technical subjects presented in conjunction with Imaginology, a series of six workshops titled "Relationship Management Technology for Global Competitive Advantage" were also conducted by John Carlisle of Transform, and Bob Parker of Parker Management Associates, Ltd.

These workshops were attended by 95 technical and commercial personnel from automobile manufacturers and their primary subassembly suppliers such as Chrysler Motors, Ford, General Motors, Volkswagen, Daewoo, Volvo, Eaton, Lear Sigler and TRW. Also in attendance were electronics manufacturers such as AT&T Microelectronics, Chrysler Acustar, Delco Electronics, Denshigiken, Ford Electronics and Microelectronics Divisions, Kanto Seiki, Motorola Pioneer and Tektronix. There were, in addition, several consultants, distributors and academics in attendance.

Following are the verbatim comments of those participants in response to the question posed at the end of the workshop:

"What does the Automobile Industry (including its prime subassembly suppliers) *need* from the Electronics Industry which it is not now getting?

And what does the Electronics Industry *need* from the Automobile Industry (and its prime subassembly suppliers) which it is not now getting?"

Each response was developed to a thoughtful level and the words chosen by the participants with some care to represent the critical essence of a point about which they felt strongly.

Following the verbatim comments as developed by the participants is a commentary by John and Bob. This commentary represents their judgement regarding the implications these comments and the surrounding discussions have for the future relationship of these two highly interdependent industries. This section also contains their conclusions as to what kind of relationship these industries will need if they are to compete successfully in a global market.

The participants' comments have been grouped into four broad headings of:

PLANNING

UNDERSTANDING

RELATIONSHIP/COMMITMENT

EXECUTION

These headings were not predetermined, but simply arose clearly as the fields in which the participants were most clearly expressing serious concerns, painful frustrations, and in some cases even heartfelt anxiety. Most of this frustration stemmed from the perceived failure or refusal of the other side to show willingness to meet what they considered to be legitimate needs.

The numbers in parentheses indicate the session in which that comment was offered:

(1)   9 a.m. Wednesday October 19
(2)   1 p.m. Wednesday October 19
(3)   10 a.m. Thursday October 20
(4)   2 p.m. Thursday October 20
(6)   2 p.m. Friday October 21

All comments which were fully developed on the flip-charts in front of all participants are included here except those from the Friday a.m. session which were inadvertently destroyed. The thoughts from that session followed the same pattern, however, and have been given proper consideration in the Implications and Conclusions Section at the end.

PLANNING

Comments from the Electronics Industry

Get the supplier into the act early enough to influence the spec (1)

Real lead time to respond to up/down scheduling (6 weeks = 6 weeks—don't ask for three weeks!) (2)

Reliable planning numbers (4)

Collaborate with us in engineering and design (4)

Early enough involvement in customer design to assure it is doable (or we can decline to supply) (6)

Comments from the Automobile Industry

Give me the *real* time (2)

Ask about our needs early on (3)

Consistent approach to problem-solving (4)

UNDERSTANDING

Comments from the Electronics Industry

Original Equipment Manufacturers understand what their application *demands*—and put that in the spec (1)

How does one become a primary supplier (especially at GM and Chrysler)? (1)

Understanding of the Automobile business (so we can work on the real *needs*)
—and buyers who *know* the real *needs* of the Automobile business (2)

Understanding of the *consumer's* needs (this can be over or under-shot)
—and buyers who *know* the consumer's real needs (2)

Tell us *why* you need it that way (3)

More Electronics Industry comments (on UNDERSTANDING)

Educate us on where you are going (3)

Listen to us (*hear* us) (3)

Visibility of user intentions (4)

Help us test our understanding of what "you" (Automobile Companies) mean (4)

Use us as a sounding board to help you define your problem (4)

Comments from the Automobile Industry (on UNDERSTANDING)

Total quality mindset—i.e. special versus common cause (1)

Understand the Electronics Industry (1)
(ed. note: yes, the plea was for the Electronics Industry to understand itself better, and *then* pass that understanding to the Automobile Industry)

Understand the final consumer's use/need (1)

Supplier to understand own internal capability (2)

Understand *Automotive* electronics (2)

Understand *my* organization (2)

Correct interpretation of data (4)

Solutions to be asked for on the basis of a shared perception of the problem (4)

Open up to J.I.T. (6)

RELATIONSHIP/COMMITMENT

Comments from the Electronics Industry

Stand behind your commitment (1)

Take a more interdependent view of the economic exchange (3)

A true commitment to programs (4)

Involve yourself in our total systems (6)

Less bullying and more cooperation (6)

Comments from the Automobile Industry (RELATIONSHIP/COMMITMENT)

Deal in good faith (2)

Be more willing to put improvements of products in, especially domestic suppliers (3)

More openness in price factors, etc. (3)

Give us the *downs* (ed.—in material cost movement) as well as the *ups* (3)

Commitment (4)

Shorter lead times (6)

System involvement (6)

Work better with your competition on Automobile Industry problems (6)

EXECUTION

Comments from the Electronics Industry

Delivery on time in die form (1)

Give us schedules we can accept/meet (6)

Comments from the Automobile Industry

Timely service—including technical and defect information, etc. (3)

Stick to your schedule (if there is fat, tell us) (6)

IMPLICATIONS AS SEEN BY CARLISLE AND PARKER

The situation now (lack of commitment to a relationship) is such that, if it continues in this direction, both industries will be increasingly unable to respond to the consumer's expectations as well as the consumer's demands.

This is because the poor quality of the individual relationships will increasingly suppress the creativity and the willingness essential for timely response.

It was clear from the discussions that the poor relationship between the two industries grows primarily from lack of trust. We perceive that this lack of trust has grown from two major sources:

- too many cases where one party or the other has not performed as agreed. In some cases this has been exacerbated by the apparent lack of concern for the consequences to the other party.

- *lack of confidence in their own commitment to sustain the relationship required.*

CONCLUSIONS OF CARLISE AND PARKER

(1)   today, planning and execution are a function of the relationship
(2)   the healthier the relationship, the more likely the early involvement and the more likely a successful execution
(3)   this is because a *good* relationship motivates both partners to be interested in the other's needs

(4)   this leads to an enlightened involvement in the real world of the other party
(5)   the key to arriving at point (4) above is to begin to put TRUST back into the relationship
(6)   this begins by ensuring successful implementations of all *promised* performance on both sides
(7)   individuals cannot, by themselves, deliver successful implementations of the complex promises needed to respond competitively to today's ultimate consumer
(8)   individuals need to find and better utilize the groups within their own organizations which are collectively empowered to assure absolutely faithful execution of all promised performance
(9)   management in both industries needs to create the conditions needed to make point (8) possible.

JOHN A. CARLISLE
ROBERT C. PARKER
October 22, 1988

Index

Note that italicized page numbers indicate that diagrams appear within the reference; 'e' denotes an epigraph.